Be Smart

with

Retirement

How I Retired Rich, Kept More Money, and Legally Paid
Zero Taxes

Morgan Carrington

Disclaimer

This book is for informational and educational purposes only. The author is not a financial advisor, tax professional, or investment consultant. The strategies, examples, and opinions presented are based on personal experience and research but should not be considered professional financial, legal, or tax advice.

Readers are encouraged to conduct their own due diligence and consult with licensed professionals before making any financial, legal, or investment decisions. The author and publisher disclaim any liability for losses or damages resulting from the use or misuse of the information contained in this book.

Table of Contents

Introduction

You have been working hard, saving diligently, and often feeling the weight of financial uncertainty. I remember when I first started setting aside even a small amount from my paycheck, unsure if that effort would ever lead to a secure future. You may be questioning whether your sacrifices and careful budgeting will provide you with the freedom to retire early and live comfortably, without the constant worry of taxes reducing your savings.

In this book, you will learn how everyday decisions can become powerful steps toward building a solid foundation for a tax-free retirement. Your journey to financial freedom starts with understanding the real impact of your financial habits and recognizing that every smart decision, no matter how small, moves you closer to your goals.

There was a time when I felt overwhelmed by the many financial choices before me. I experienced moments of doubt, wondering if I was making the right decisions with my money. It was during those challenging periods that I discovered strategies to reduce my tax burden, enabling me to reinvest in my future. You might be facing similar struggles, feeling that the system is set against you.

This book is here to show you that the system can be managed with the right knowledge and techniques. With determination and careful planning, you can build a future where financial freedom is within reach.

Why "Pay Zero" Matters: Rethinking Taxes in Retirement

For many, the idea of a tax-free retirement feels out of reach. Taxes are often viewed as an inevitable cost that continuously takes a portion of your income. I once believed that taxes were an unavoidable expense—a drain that diminished the results of my hard work. However, as I learned more about effective tax strategies and smart financial planning, I realized that you can structure your retirement so that your income is not burdened by high taxes, and in some cases, you might even pay zero taxes.

Achieving a tax-free retirement means keeping more of the money you earn, which gives you greater control over your future. Imagine waking up each day knowing that your income is yours to use as you wish, free from the worry of tax deductions. This approach is not about shirking responsibilities but about planning wisely so that your money works for you without unnecessary drains. It is a shift in perspective that allows you to focus on long-term growth and stability rather than being caught up in short-term losses.

Overview & How to Use This Book

This book is designed as a practical guide that you can use to build a retirement plan tailored to your unique situation. Each chapter offers actionable advice, real-life examples, and step-by-step strategies to help you reduce or eliminate the tax burden on your retirement income. The layout of the book makes it simple to follow the guidance and apply the lessons to your own life without feeling overwhelmed by technical language.

As you progress through the chapters, you will encounter various tools and techniques that have proven effective for me and many others who have achieved early retirement with a tax-free income. I share personal experiences throughout this book to inspire you and remind you that you are not alone in this journey. My aim is to speak directly to you, using clear and relatable examples from my own life, to help you build confidence in your financial decisions.

Every section builds on the last, providing you with a clear roadmap from understanding basic principles to implementing advanced strategies. You will find checklists, practical exercises, and resource recommendations to help you track your progress and make informed decisions along the way. Treat this book as your reference guide—a tool to return to whenever you need clarity or a boost of confidence in your planning.

Chapter 1

The Early Retirement Mindset

This chapter sets the stage for a new way of thinking about your financial future. You are not simply planning for a retirement that comes with restrictions and endless waiting. Instead, you are learning to build a life where your hard work translates into true freedom.

In these pages, you will discover what financial freedom really means, how to set practical goals, and the methods to break down the mental barriers that often keep you from achieving early retirement. You will find that each step you take is part of a larger strategy that empowers you to take control of your income and future lifestyle.

The insights shared here are drawn from real experiences and tested strategies that have helped many reach a state of financial independence. I have faced many challenges and moments of uncertainty myself, and I want you to know that every obstacle you encounter is an opportunity to learn and grow stronger. Your journey is unique, and the principles outlined in this chapter are designed to support you regardless of your starting point.

As you read, reflect on your own financial habits, your aspirations, and the vision you have for a life free from the burdens of unnecessary taxes. This chapter invites you to rethink the way you approach money, work, and leisure. It is a call to shift your mindset so that you can build a secure, fulfilling retirement that lets you enjoy the freedom you deserve.

Defining Financial Freedom

Financial freedom is the state in which you have enough income from your investments and savings to support your lifestyle without being forced to work for a paycheck. It is about creating a situation where your money works for you, generating steady returns and allowing you to live on your own terms. When you achieve financial freedom, you are not bound by the demands of a traditional job or limited by the stress of covering monthly bills.

Instead, you experience a sense of security and independence that opens up a range of opportunities. You are free to choose projects that excite you, spend more time with family and friends, and pursue interests that truly matter.

In my own journey, reaching a point where I did not worry about every expense was a turning point. I realized that financial freedom was not about earning a high salary alone, but about managing resources wisely, investing strategically, and planning for the long term. Your path to financial freedom starts with small steps, such as reducing debt and setting up automated savings, which gradually build the foundation for a secure future. Every mindful decision adds up to lasting change. Start small, grow big today.

Defining financial freedom means more than simply having an abundant bank balance. It is about having the flexibility to decide how you spend your time and whom you spend it with.

You see, when I first started working, I measured success by the number of hours I logged at the office, not by the freedom I experienced outside work. I quickly learned that a high salary does not always translate into security if you are overwhelmed by expenses and obligations.

Financial freedom is achieved when your income from passive sources covers your essential needs and supports your lifestyle choices without forcing you to trade time for money. It means having the power to take a break without the stress of financial strain, to pursue creative projects without worrying about how to pay the bills, and to live a life where your priorities come first.

You might recall moments when you felt trapped by a job that did not offer you the time or energy to enjoy life. I remember feeling frustrated and confined by the relentless cycle of work, debt, and stress. At that time, the idea of early retirement seemed like a distant dream. Now, by making smart choices and optimizing how I manage my resources, I have reached a point where money is a tool for freedom rather than a source of anxiety.

This broader definition of financial freedom shifts your focus from simply accumulating wealth to embracing a lifestyle where your assets actively support your dreams. It challenges you to rethink your relationship with money and to prioritize long-term security over short-term indulgence. With this perspective, you begin to see every investment and saving decision as a step toward a more liberated future.

Every clear choice builds the foundation for a truly independent life. By taking time to reflect on your values and ambitions, you unlock the potential to create a personalized plan that fits your life. Every decision, from small savings to major investments, becomes a stepping stone on your path. You deserve a future where your financial choices empower you to live fully and freely. Every mindful choice builds a brighter, more secure tomorrow for you.

Your journey toward financial freedom is deeply personal and requires a clear understanding of what matters most to you. It is essential to align your financial goals with your personal values and life ambitions. When you define financial freedom in your own terms, you create a roadmap that reflects your unique priorities and dreams. I have learned that the path is not the same for everyone. Some of us prioritize travel and exploration, while others focus on security and a comfortable home life.

By defining what freedom means to you, you can tailor your financial strategies to support the lifestyle you truly desire. This process may involve making tough decisions about spending habits and saving practices, but every choice you make is a building block toward the future you envision.

Embracing this mindset shifts your focus from immediate gratification to long-term benefits. It also inspires you to seek out opportunities that enhance your overall quality of life. Your actions today will set the stage for tomorrow, ensuring that each step brings you closer to a reality where you are in charge of your own destiny.

By taking time to reflect on your values and ambitions, you unlock the potential to create a personalized plan that fits your life. Every decision, from small savings to major investments, becomes a stepping stone on your path. You deserve a future where your financial choices empower you to live fully and freely. Every mindful choice builds a brighter, more secure tomorrow for you. Keep refining your vision and remain persistent; each improvement in your plan brings you one step closer to a life of complete financial independence.

As you define what financial freedom means for you, keep in mind that this state is not an unreachable ideal but a practical goal attainable through disciplined planning and smart choices. Every investment decision, every saving habit, and every calculated risk contributes to building a future where work becomes optional.

The steps you take today lay the groundwork for a lifetime of opportunities. Reflect on your progress regularly and adjust your strategies as your circumstances evolve. Financial freedom is a journey that requires commitment, learning, and persistence. With each wise decision, you move closer to a life where you are in charge, free from the constant pressures of financial worry.

Embrace this process with confidence, knowing that your efforts are paving the way for lasting independence. Remember that every choice plays a significant role in constructing a future where you are free to live on your terms.

Setting Goals and Creating a Vision

Setting clear goals is the first step towards a successful journey to early retirement and tax-free income. When you define your objectives, you establish a roadmap that guides your actions and decisions every day. Goals transform abstract dreams into actionable plans.

I recall a time when my aspirations were vague, and I struggled to see the connection between my daily habits and the long-term freedom I craved. It was only after I set specific targets for saving, investing, and reducing expenses that I began to understand the power of focused effort. You will find that establishing measurable goals brings clarity and motivation to your financial journey. Each goal acts as a milestone, marking progress along the path to financial independence.

Whether you aim to save a certain amount each month, achieve a particular investment return, or reduce your spending by a set percentage, clear objectives provide a sense of direction and purpose. This approach makes the challenging process of building a secure retirement more manageable and less overwhelming.

When your goals are well-defined, you can break them down into smaller, achievable steps that lead to consistent progress. This process also enables you to monitor your performance, adjust your strategies when necessary, and celebrate your accomplishments along the way. In essence, setting goals is not just about numbers on a page; it is about creating a vision for the life you want to live. It is a commitment to yourself that every effort counts and that success is within your reach.

By writing down your goals and reviewing them regularly, you create a tangible reminder of what you are working toward. Every step forward, no matter how small, reinforces your commitment and builds momentum. This practice transforms vague dreams into a clear plan, energizing you to make progress each day steadily.

Once you have set your goals, the next step is to outline a clear strategy to achieve them. This means breaking down large targets into smaller, manageable tasks. I remember a period when I faced the overwhelming challenge of saving enough money for early retirement. I began by setting a modest monthly savings goal and tracking every expense.

Over time, these small actions accumulated, and I was able to see tangible results that motivated me to aim higher. You will learn that discipline in your daily financial habits is the cornerstone of success. Writing down your priorities, creating a budget, and monitoring your progress are not just routine activities—they are essential tools that help you stay on track.

By mapping out your financial journey step by step, you can identify areas where you might need to adjust your plans. A detailed strategy helps you prepare for unexpected expenses and market changes, ensuring that you remain resilient in the face of challenges.

Remember that every milestone achieved is a testament to your hard work and commitment. In this process, patience and persistence are as valuable as any financial technique. Trust that your efforts will lead to meaningful outcomes, and let each small victory propel you toward the larger goals you have set for your future. Develop a habit of reviewing your strategy regularly.

Write down your progress, celebrate your milestones, and adjust your plans when necessary. Each review reinforces your commitment and sharpens your focus. Your dedication to these small steps will gradually create a solid foundation for a prosperous future, ultimately leading you to early retirement with the freedom you have always dreamed about. Keep refining your vision and remain persistent; each improvement in your plan brings you one step closer to a life of complete financial independence.

Creating a vision for your future is a powerful exercise that complements your goal setting. This vision is not a vague fantasy but a detailed and realistic picture of the life you wish to lead. When you write down what your ideal retirement looks like, you give shape to your ambitions.

I remember the moment when I first put my vision on paper. I listed everything from the kind of home I wanted to live in to the activities I longed to pursue during my days off. That process made my aspirations tangible and provided a constant reminder of why I was working so hard. Your vision should include both financial targets and lifestyle goals. It may involve traveling to new places, dedicating more time to hobbies, or simply having the freedom to relax and enjoy life without financial constraints.

As you articulate your vision, be honest about what matters most to you. This clarity will help you maintain focus even when challenges arise. Writing down your vision serves as both a motivational tool and a blueprint for action. Over time, as you achieve your milestones, your vision may evolve. Update it regularly to reflect your growth and changing priorities.

Remember, a clear vision empowers you to make decisions that align with your long-term goals. It reinforces your commitment and gives you the courage to take bold steps towards early retirement. In crafting your vision, you lay the foundation for a future where every decision contributes to a secure, fulfilling life.

Keep this vision visible by writing it down and revisiting it frequently. Let it serve as a daily reminder of the promising future you are working to create. Your vision will evolve, but its core purpose remains the same. Stay focused, remain determined.

Overcoming Mental Barriers to Early Retirement

Mental barriers are often the most challenging obstacles on the path to early retirement. These barriers can take the form of fear, self-doubt, or deeply ingrained beliefs that tell you it is too risky or impossible to achieve a tax-free, independent future.

Many times, you may hear a voice in your head insisting that you are not capable of managing your finances effectively or that unforeseen circumstances will always derail your plans. I have experienced this inner critic during moments of uncertainty, feeling as if every step I took was fraught with risk. Such negative thoughts can prevent you from taking the necessary actions that lead to success.

It is important to recognize these mental blocks and understand that they are not facts but perceptions that can be changed. When you challenge these beliefs, you open the door to new possibilities. Accept that the journey toward early retirement is not a straight line; it is filled with setbacks, learning opportunities, and occasional failures. Rather than letting fear paralyze you, use it as a signal to prepare better and work smarter.

Understand that every successful person has faced doubts and obstacles along the way. Your mind can be your greatest asset if you train it to focus on potential and progress instead of limitations.

Acknowledging your fears is the first step to overcoming them, and with time and practice, you can replace these doubts with a mindset geared toward growth and achievement. Take a moment to write down your fears and question their validity. Realize that many of these worries stem from past experiences rather than future realities. Embrace the idea that you can learn from mistakes and improve with every effort you make. Write your fears on paper, then let them go, knowing you are stronger than your doubts indeed.

Overcoming these mental barriers requires a change in your thought patterns and habits. I remember a time when the fear of failure kept me from taking risks that could have advanced my financial goals. Every time I hesitated, I lost an opportunity to grow and learn.

To overcome this, I started practicing mindfulness and positive self-talk, techniques that helped me shift my focus from what might go wrong to what could go right. You can adopt these strategies by setting aside a few minutes each day to reflect on your accomplishments and remind yourself of your strengths. Surround yourself with people who inspire you and challenge negative beliefs. Replace doubt with practical planning and actionable steps. Instead of letting the possibility of failure stop you, view each setback as a lesson that brings you closer to success. Your journey is filled with moments of trial, but with every challenge, you have the chance to improve and refine your approach. The more you practice these new habits, the more natural they will become, eventually overpowering the old, limiting beliefs.

Remember that mental resilience is built over time through persistent effort and self-compassion. Every step you take to silence the inner critic reinforces your determination and increases your confidence in your financial journey. I began to notice that every small victory over my doubts built a reservoir of strength. I kept a journal of my successes and reminders of my abilities, which gradually quieted the negative voices. This consistent practice helped me transform fear into a catalyst for action, inspiring me to take risks with a calm mind and a clear focus on my goals.

Regularly, remind yourself that overcoming mental barriers is a process that strengthens your resolve and sharpens your ability to achieve financial success. Keep moving forward each day.

To turn your mindset from a source of doubt into a driver of achievement, it is vital to implement actionable techniques. Start by setting aside regular time to reflect on your progress and update your goals. Create a list of affirmations that remind you of your strengths and past successes. I have found that writing these affirmations on sticky notes and placing them around my workspace helps maintain a positive outlook during challenging times.

When negative thoughts creep in, pause, breathe, and recite these positive statements to reset your focus. Embrace the idea that setbacks are temporary and that each obstacle presents a chance to learn something new. In moments of self-doubt, reach out to a mentor or trusted friend who can offer objective advice and encouragement. Overcoming mental barriers is a continuous process, one that requires patience and resilience. Every time you replace a negative thought with a constructive one, you reinforce a habit that will support your journey towards early retirement. Keep a record of these instances to remind yourself of your progress. As you build this habit, you will notice that challenges become less daunting and your ability to act decisively improves.

Your mindset, once held captive by fear and uncertainty, will transform into a powerful asset that drives your financial success and personal growth. Focus on cultivating a growth mindset by regularly challenging your limiting beliefs. Write down any negative thoughts and actively replace them with positive, actionable statements.

This deliberate practice will gradually build mental strength and allow you to face challenges with increased confidence and clarity. Every effort you make in overcoming self-doubt reinforces your resilience. Remember, each small victory in shifting your mindset is a critical step towards securing the retirement you desire. Stay committed and always.

Chapter 2

Demystifying Taxes

This chapter breaks down the complex subject of taxes and shows you how they affect your wealth, the common misunderstandings many people have about taxation, and the fundamental tax rules that every investor should know. In this chapter, you will learn how taxes can erode your hard-earned money if you are not careful and how understanding the rules can actually work in your favor. I want you to feel empowered by knowledge—when you know how the system works, you are better able to design your financial future in a way that minimizes tax costs and maximizes growth. Let's start by looking at how taxes impact your wealth, then clear up some widespread myths, and finally, explain the basics of tax law for investors like you.

How Taxes Impact Your Wealth

Taxes are a reality of life, and they affect every aspect of your financial journey. When you earn money, whether through employment, investments, or other sources, a portion of it is subject to tax. This means that the income you bring home is always less than the gross amount you earn. The more you earn, the more you might be required to pay, and if you are not careful, taxes can significantly reduce the wealth you accumulate over time.

I remember the first time I saw a tax return statement that detailed every deduction and credit. It felt overwhelming, and I questioned how something designed to be a public service could seem so complicated. You might have felt the same way at some point. It is not unusual to feel frustrated by the complexity of tax laws and the impression that they are stacked against your financial goals. However, understanding the way taxes work can be a turning point in your financial planning.

Every dollar you earn has the potential to grow if it is managed wisely. When you factor in taxes, that potential can shrink dramatically if you ignore the impact of tax liabilities. For instance, if you invest in an account where gains are taxed annually, you might end up paying a significant amount of tax on your profits before you even reach retirement age. This means that even if your investments perform well, the real value of your gains is less than what you see on paper.

Let's say you earn an annual return of 8% on your investments. If you are in a high tax bracket, a substantial portion of those returns might be lost to taxes, reducing the effective return to a much lower rate. On the other hand, if you learn how to use tax-advantaged accounts or structure your investments in a tax-efficient manner, you can keep more of your money working for you. I recall a period in my early investment years when I ignored tax planning; my returns were consistently reduced by unexpected tax bills. It was a wake-up call that made me change my strategy to include tax planning as a core component of my investment process.

For you, understanding the impact of taxes on your wealth is the first step toward making informed decisions. When you plan your investments, you must account for the long-term tax implications. Whether it is through choosing tax-deferred accounts, tax-free savings options, or by timing the sale of assets to minimize capital gains tax, every decision matters. By being proactive, you can reduce the tax drag on your portfolio and ensure that more of your money remains invested and compounding over time.

Taxes also affect different sources of income in various ways. Wages, dividends, interest, and capital gains are all taxed at different rates, and some income may be subject to additional taxes like the alternative minimum tax. For example, long-term capital gains are often taxed at a lower rate than ordinary income, which means that holding an investment for a longer period can sometimes be more beneficial from a tax standpoint. This is a powerful strategy you can use if you plan carefully.

Furthermore, many people underestimate the cumulative effect of taxes over decades. Even a small difference in the effective tax rate can result in a substantial difference in the final amount of wealth accumulated. The power of compounding does not just work on your returns—it also works against you when taxes are involved. A seemingly minor tax expense today can become a major obstacle over a long period.

That is why understanding how taxes impact your wealth is crucial; it gives you the opportunity to plan in a way that mitigates these costs and helps you reach your retirement goals faster.

When you view your finances through the lens of tax impact, every investment decision becomes more strategic. It's not just about making money—it's about keeping as much of that money as possible. Taxes can be a hidden cost that eats away at your portfolio, but by making informed choices, you can shield yourself from unnecessary tax burdens. As you move forward, always ask yourself: "How will this decision affect my tax situation?" This habit will become one of your most valuable tools in building and preserving wealth.

Common Misconceptions About Taxation

There are many myths about taxes that can lead you to make poor financial decisions. One common misconception is that taxes are an unavoidable penalty on your income. You might think that no matter what you do, the government will always take a significant portion of your earnings, leaving you with little room for growth. While it is true that taxes are part of life, you have more control over them than you might realize.

Many people assume that all tax-advantaged accounts are the same or that they automatically lead to a better retirement outcome. I once believed that simply putting money into any retirement account was enough to secure my future. Over time, I discovered that the details matter—a lot. For example, not all tax-deferred accounts work the same way when it comes to withdrawals or required distributions, and some might expose you to higher taxes later on. You might have heard stories from friends or family who ended up with large tax bills even after years of saving diligently. These stories are often rooted in misunderstandings about how the tax code operates.

Another myth is that tax planning is only for the wealthy or financial experts. You may think that if you are not earning a high income or managing a large portfolio, tax planning is not a priority.

In reality, every financial decision you make is affected by taxes, regardless of your income level. When I was starting out, I assumed that my modest income meant I did not need to worry about complex tax strategies. It wasn't until I reviewed my finances more carefully that I saw how even small tax liabilities were holding me back. Once I began to learn and apply basic tax strategies, I was able to keep more of my money and put it to work for my future.

Another common belief is that the tax code is intentionally designed to be confusing and that there is little you can do about it. While the tax system does have its complexities, it is not impenetrable. With the right resources and a willingness to learn, you can understand the rules that affect your investments and income. I recall spending many evenings poring over guides and speaking with financial advisors to understand how to reduce my tax burden. You have the same opportunity. The more you know, the better you can shape your financial strategies to work with the tax system rather than against it.

There is also a tendency to think that all income is taxed at the same rate, which is not true. The tax system offers different treatments for various types of income. For instance, income earned from wages is usually taxed at a higher rate than income generated from long-term investments. Many people are unaware that by strategically timing the sale of assets or by holding investments for a longer period, they can benefit from lower tax rates on capital gains. This misunderstanding can lead to decisions that end up costing you more in taxes than necessary.

A further misconception is that tax deductions and credits are only for those with complex financial situations. You might feel that if you have a straightforward income stream, you do not have to worry about these opportunities.

However, deductions and credits are available to a wide range of taxpayers, and learning how to use them can make a real difference in your overall tax liability. I once overlooked several small deductions simply because I thought they wouldn't add up to much. Over time, I learned that every little bit counts, and those small savings accumulated into a significant amount when applied over the long term.

It is important for you to dispel these myths early on. By recognizing that tax planning is not reserved for a select few, you open the door to making choices that help you keep more of your earnings.

Tax planning is a vital part of building wealth, and when you set aside time to learn the basics, you empower yourself to take control of your financial future. The more accurately you understand how taxes work, the better you can plan to minimize their impact and maximize your returns. Each step you take in clarifying these common misconceptions brings you closer to achieving a tax-efficient retirement.

Don't let fear or confusion hold you back from exploring practical tax strategies. Instead, see this as an opportunity to educate yourself and transform your approach to money management. Once you start to see taxes as a manageable part of your financial plan, you can focus on the strategies that will lead to lasting wealth. You deserve to have a clear understanding of your financial landscape, and that begins with correcting the myths that have held you back.

The Basics of Tax Law for Investors

For investors, the tax code can seem like a complicated maze, but getting a handle on the basics is essential for protecting and growing your wealth. The first step is to understand the different types of taxes that apply to investment income and how they can affect your overall returns.

Income Taxes and Investment Income

When you earn income from investments, such as dividends or interest, that income is typically taxed at your ordinary income tax rate. This rate can be significantly higher than the rates applied to long-term capital gains, which are earned when you sell an asset that you have held for more than a year. For you, this means that holding investments for a longer period can often result in a lower tax rate on the gains. I remember being surprised when I learned that selling an investment too soon could result in paying a higher tax rate. This realization prompted me to adjust my strategy, and over time, the benefits of a long-term approach became clear.

Capital Gains Taxes

Capital gains taxes are the taxes you pay on the profit from the sale of an asset. The rate at which these gains are taxed depends on how long you hold the asset. Short-term capital gains, which are gains on assets held for less than a year, are taxed as ordinary income. In contrast, long-term capital gains enjoy a lower tax rate, which can make a significant difference over time. Understanding this difference is crucial for planning your investment strategy. You might decide to hold onto investments longer to benefit from these lower rates, even if it means delaying the sale of an asset that has performed well in the short term.

Tax-Advantaged Accounts

One of the most powerful tools in your financial arsenal is the use of tax-advantaged accounts. These include retirement accounts such as IRAs and 401(k)s, as well as other investment vehicles like Health Savings Accounts (HSAs). Money held in these accounts grows either tax-deferred or tax-free, depending on the type of account. For example, with a Roth IRA, you pay taxes on your contributions now, but all the growth and withdrawals in retirement are tax-free. I recall the moment I first contributed to a Roth IRA and realized that it was not just a retirement account, but a means to shelter my investment growth from future taxes. When you take advantage of these accounts, you can maximize your savings and reduce the long-term impact of taxes on your wealth.

Understanding Tax Brackets and Deductions

Tax brackets are the ranges of income that are taxed at different rates. As your income increases, you move into higher tax brackets, which means that additional income is taxed at a higher rate. This is why managing your taxable income is crucial for keeping your tax bill under control. Many investors are not aware of the potential benefits of strategically timing income or deductions to avoid jumping into a higher tax bracket unnecessarily. By planning your income and expenses, you can sometimes shift income to years when your tax rate is lower.

Deductions and credits are another critical aspect of tax law. Deductions reduce your taxable income, while credits reduce the amount of tax you owe directly. Learning which deductions you qualify for—such as those related to education, homeownership, or certain investments—can help reduce your overall tax liability. I learned the hard way that overlooking available deductions could cost you more money than you might expect. Over time, I made it a point to review my financial situation every year with a tax professional, ensuring that I was not missing any opportunities to reduce my taxable income.

Tax Reporting and Compliance

Another important area for investors is understanding how to report your investment income correctly. The IRS requires you to report all sources of income, and mistakes in your tax return can lead to penalties or even audits. While it might seem tedious, accurate reporting is a key part of managing your finances responsibly. In my early years as an investor, I once received a notice from the IRS because I had misreported a dividend. That experience taught me the importance of keeping meticulous records and reviewing my tax documents carefully each year.

Planning for Future Tax Changes

The tax code is not static—it changes over time. New laws can affect how much tax you pay on your investments and what strategies work best for reducing your tax burden. For you, staying informed about potential changes in tax policy is an essential part of maintaining a tax-efficient investment strategy. I remember feeling frustrated when tax law changes meant that a strategy, I had relied on no longer provided the benefits I expected. However, by staying flexible and continuously educating yourself, you can adjust your plan to keep pace with evolving regulations.

Putting It All Together

Understanding the basics of tax law is not just about knowing the numbers—it is about integrating that knowledge into your overall investment strategy. When you have a clear grasp of how income is taxed, how capital gains work, and which accounts offer tax advantages, you can make decisions that preserve your wealth and accelerate your progress toward a tax-free retirement. I learned that effective tax planning requires a combination of good record-keeping, regular review of your financial situation, and the willingness to update your strategy as circumstances change.

This means taking a proactive approach. It is not enough to simply earn returns on your investments; you must also be mindful of the tax implications of every decision. By planning ahead and using the tax rules to your advantage, you can reduce the amount of tax that eats into your gains and help your money work harder over time. Each time you adjust your strategy, you are reinforcing your commitment to achieving a secure financial future where taxes do not stand in the way of your goals.

This chapter has provided you with a clear look at how taxes impact your wealth, cleared up common misunderstandings about taxation, and explained the basics of tax law for investors. When you take the time to learn and apply these principles, you set yourself up for a future where your financial decisions work in your favor. With this knowledge, you are better prepared to design an investment strategy that minimizes tax costs and maximizes growth, bringing you one step closer to a tax-free retirement.

Embrace the power of knowledge in your financial journey. Every decision you make, from the types of accounts you use to the timing of your investments, plays a role in how much of your money you get to keep. With a solid understanding of tax fundamentals, you are empowered to keep more of your hard-earned money and use it to build a secure, independent future. Keep learning, keep adjusting, and let your informed choices guide you to lasting financial freedom.

Chapter 3

Maximizing Tax-Advantaged Accounts

This chapter is dedicated to showing you how to make the most of tax-advantaged accounts to secure your financial future. You will learn about the various retirement vehicles available, such as Roth IRAs, Traditional IRAs, 401(k)s, and more. We will discuss strategies to leverage employer-sponsored plans and provide guidance on choosing the right account that fits your personal financial goals. Through personal stories and practical examples, you will gain a clear understanding of how these accounts work and how you can use them to build tax-free income for early retirement.

Overview of Retirement Vehicles

When you set out to build a secure financial future, tax-advantaged accounts are among the most powerful tools available to you. These accounts not only help your investments grow faster by deferring or even eliminating taxes, but they also provide structure and discipline to your saving habits.

Roth IRA

The Roth IRA is an account where you pay taxes on your contributions upfront, and your withdrawals in retirement are tax-free. You might find this option especially appealing if you expect to be in a higher tax bracket when you retire or if you want the flexibility to withdraw your money without a tax hit later on. I remember when I first opened my Roth IRA; I was struck by the simplicity of paying taxes now to secure tax-free growth for the future.

You, too, can take comfort in knowing that every dollar you contribute grows without the worry of future tax deductions. With the Roth IRA, your retirement savings can compound over decades without being eroded by taxes when you finally withdraw the funds. This account is a favorite for those who plan to retire early and want full access to their funds without penalty in later years.

Traditional IRA

In contrast, the Traditional IRA allows you to contribute pre-tax dollars, lowering your taxable income in the year you contribute. Taxes are paid later, when you withdraw the funds in retirement. This vehicle can be a strategic choice if you expect to be in a lower tax bracket after you retire. I once met a friend who meticulously planned her contributions to her Traditional IRA, choosing to postpone tax payments until her retirement years when her income—and therefore her tax rate—would be lower. You might find that this approach works well if you prefer to reduce your current tax burden and plan to rely on a steady income in retirement. The key with a Traditional IRA is to balance the benefit of reducing your taxable income today against the possibility of paying taxes on a larger sum later. In both types of IRAs, you are rewarded with tax-deferred or tax-free growth, allowing your money to work for you over the long term.

401(k) Plans

Employer-sponsored 401(k) plans are another cornerstone of retirement planning. With a 401(k), you often contribute through payroll deductions, and many employers offer matching contributions, which is essentially free money added to your account. I remember the excitement I felt the first time I saw my employer's match deposited into my 401(k). It was a clear signal that my company was invested in my future. You have the opportunity to maximize these benefits by contributing at least enough to receive the full match offered by your employer.

The tax advantages of a 401(k) come in two forms: you can choose between a Traditional 401(k), which works like a Traditional IRA with pre-tax contributions, or a Roth 401(k), where you pay taxes on contributions upfront. Each option has its benefits depending on your current tax situation and expected retirement income. What makes the 401(k) plan so compelling is not only the immediate tax break (or tax-free withdrawals in the case of the Roth 401(k)) but also the disciplined savings plan that helps you build wealth systematically over time.

Other Vehicles

Beyond the main accounts, there are additional tax-advantaged vehicles that you might explore. Health Savings Accounts (HSAs), for instance, offer triple tax advantages—contributions are tax-deductible, growth is tax-free, and withdrawals for qualified medical expenses are not taxed. Although HSAs are designed for healthcare costs, many people use them as an additional retirement savings tool.

Another option is the SEP IRA, typically used by self-employed individuals, which allows for high contribution limits. If you run your own business or work as a freelancer, these accounts can help you save a significant portion of your earnings in a tax-efficient manner. Each of these accounts has its own rules and benefits, and understanding how they work can open up new opportunities for you to keep more of your money and grow your nest egg efficiently.

Strategies to Leverage Employer-Sponsored Plans

Employer-sponsored plans, particularly 401(k) accounts, offer unique advantages that you can use to your benefit. When your employer matches your contributions, you are effectively receiving an immediate return on your investment. This match is not something you can easily replicate through other investments, so it's crucial to make it a priority in your overall savings strategy.

Maximizing the Employer Match

One of the simplest ways to boost your retirement savings is to contribute enough to get the full employer match. Many employers will match contributions up to a certain percentage of your salary. I recall a time when I was tempted to invest less than the maximum, thinking that a little extra cash in my paycheck was appealing. However, after learning about the significant benefits of the employer match, I made it a point to adjust my contributions. You should also aim to contribute at least the minimum required to get that free money. The match is an instant gain that directly increases your retirement fund without any extra cost to you. By ensuring that you contribute enough to get the full match, you are setting a solid foundation for your long-term savings.

Timing and Contribution Adjustments

Another strategy involves timing your contributions wisely throughout the year. If your employer offers annual or semi-annual bonuses or if there is a specific enrollment period, use those opportunities to boost your contributions. I once had a year when I received a significant bonus; instead of spending it all, I directed a large portion into my 401(k). This not only increased my retirement savings but also reduced my taxable income for that year. You can apply similar strategies by reviewing your income and planning contributions when you expect to have extra cash. Even small increases in your contribution rate can add up over time, thanks to the power of compounding.

Taking Advantage of Automatic Increases

Some employers offer an automatic escalation feature for your 401(k) contributions, gradually increasing the amount you save each year. This method makes saving easier by eliminating the need for manual adjustments and helps you keep up with rising living costs. I remember setting up automatic increases and feeling a sense of relief, knowing that

I was steadily working toward my retirement goals without having to constantly rethink my budget. This feature can be especially beneficial if you find it challenging to make frequent adjustments to your savings plan. When you let the system work for you, your savings grow almost effortlessly, and you are more likely to meet your long-term objectives.

Evaluating Fees and Investment Options

Employer-sponsored plans vary not only in the matching contributions but also in the fees and investment options available. It is important to review the fee structure of your plan and choose the investments that align with your risk tolerance and long-term goals. I once encountered a 401(k) plan with high administrative fees that ate into my returns. After discussing it with a financial advisor and comparing options, I made a switch that significantly improved my overall performance.

You should take the time to examine the details of your plan and, if necessary, consult with a trusted expert. Understanding the fees and investment choices available in your employer-sponsored plan is critical for maximizing the benefit of these accounts. Reducing fees and selecting appropriate investments can lead to substantial savings over the years, ensuring that more of your money remains invested and grows tax-free.

Coordinating with Other Savings Strategies

Your employer-sponsored plan is one piece of a broader savings strategy. It works best when it is coordinated with other tax-advantaged accounts, such as IRAs or HSAs. I have found that integrating these different accounts into a cohesive plan creates a stronger safety net for my future. You might use your 401(k) for its match and tax-deferred growth while using a Roth IRA for its tax-free withdrawals in retirement. By combining multiple accounts, you can take advantage of the strengths of each and create a more balanced approach to saving. The key is to align your contributions in a way that maximizes the benefits of all available accounts. When you have a well-rounded savings strategy, you are better prepared to adjust to changes in income, tax law, or personal circumstances.

Employer Stock Purchase Plans (ESPPs)

Another employer-sponsored option to explore is the Employee Stock Purchase Plan (ESPP). These plans allow you to buy company stock at a discounted rate, often with favorable tax treatment if certain conditions are met. I remember the excitement of being able to invest in the company I worked for at a lower price.

However, it is important to weigh the potential risks, as putting too much of your portfolio into a single stock can reduce diversification. If your company offers an ESPP, you should evaluate how it fits into your overall investment strategy. Using the ESPP wisely can provide an additional boost to your retirement savings while offering the potential for growth if your company performs well. Just be sure to balance this with other investments to manage risk effectively.

How to Choose the Right Account for Your Goals

Choosing the right tax-advantaged account is not a one-size-fits-all decision. It requires you to take a hard look at your financial situation, your current tax bracket, your expected income in retirement, and your long-term goals. In this section, you will learn how to weigh the benefits and limitations of each option and decide which accounts to prioritize.

Assessing Your Current Tax Situation

Your present tax bracket plays a significant role in determining which type of account might serve you best. If you are in a higher tax bracket today, you might lean toward using a Roth IRA or Roth 401(k) where you pay taxes now and enjoy tax-free withdrawals later. I remember when I was earning a higher income early in my career, I found it beneficial to allocate more resources to a Roth account. This approach allowed me to lock in my current tax rate and avoid paying a higher rate later on. You should start by analyzing your income and tax obligations to decide which accounts offer the greatest benefit now and in the future.

Evaluating Your Retirement Income Expectations

Think about what your retirement income might look like. If you anticipate a lower income after you retire, a Traditional IRA or Traditional 401(k) might be more attractive because the taxes you pay on withdrawals could be lower. On the other hand, if you expect your income to remain stable or even increase in retirement, the tax-free withdrawals from a Roth account could be advantageous.

I once sat down with my financial advisor to model different retirement scenarios. The exercise helped me see that my ideal strategy involved a mix of both Traditional and Roth accounts to hedge against uncertainties. You should explore these projections and compare how each type of account affects your net income in retirement. This careful analysis will help you decide which accounts best match your financial plans.

Matching Account Benefits with Your Goals

Your goals are unique, and the right mix of accounts depends on what you want to achieve. For instance, if your goal is to retire early with complete flexibility in accessing your funds, a Roth IRA might be ideal since it offers tax-free withdrawals and fewer restrictions. In contrast, if your focus is on reducing your taxable income now and you plan to work into your later years, a Traditional 401(k) might align better with your objectives.

I recall a period when I revised my financial goals after a change in my career path. I adjusted my portfolio to emphasize accounts that would provide more immediate tax benefits, ensuring that my savings strategy matched my evolving lifestyle. You must review your goals periodically and adjust your account mix to reflect any changes in your personal or financial situation. This alignment between your objectives and your savings vehicles is critical for long-term success.

Weighing Flexibility Versus Tax Benefits

Another important aspect is the flexibility each account offers. Some accounts, such as Roth IRAs, allow you to withdraw contributions without penalty if an emergency arises. This flexibility can provide peace of mind if you face unexpected expenses. However, other accounts might offer better long-term tax benefits at the cost of more restrictions on withdrawals. I experienced a situation when unexpected costs arose, and the ability to withdraw from my Roth IRA without penalty proved to be a lifesaver. You should weigh how much flexibility you need against the potential tax advantages. It is essential to strike a balance that suits both your current lifestyle and your long-term retirement plan.

Consulting with a Professional

Choosing the right mix of tax-advantaged accounts can be complex, and sometimes a discussion with a financial advisor can provide clarity. I have found that even a single session with a trusted professional helped me see details that I had overlooked. If you are uncertain, investing in professional advice can pay dividends in the long run. A financial expert can help you run the numbers, explain the trade-offs, and recommend an approach tailored to your situation. You should not hesitate to seek guidance if you feel overwhelmed by the choices. Taking the time to consult with an expert can ensure that you are making informed decisions that align with your goals.

Building a Diversified Strategy

Ultimately, the goal is to build a diversified strategy that uses multiple tax-advantaged accounts to protect your wealth from unnecessary taxes. You might decide to use a combination of Roth IRAs, Traditional IRAs, and employer-sponsored 401(k) plans to capture both current and future tax benefits. I remember when I first structured my retirement portfolio with a mix of these accounts; it provided a sense of balance and security. By spreading your savings across different vehicles, you reduce the risk that a change in tax laws or personal circumstances will undermine your overall plan. This diversified approach is a practical way to shield yourself from uncertainty while maximizing growth. You have the opportunity to adjust the proportions over time as your income, tax situation, and goals evolve.

Reviewing and Adjusting Over Time

As you move through different stages of your career and life, your priorities may shift. What worked well in your twenties might not be the best strategy in your forties or fifties. I have revisited my account allocations several times over the years to ensure that my strategy remains aligned with my current circumstances. You should plan to review your retirement accounts periodically and adjust your contributions if needed. This proactive management will keep your savings strategy robust and responsive to changes in tax policy or personal goals. Regular reviews and adjustments are essential components of a successful long-term plan.

Maximizing tax-advantaged accounts is a critical element in building a secure and tax-free retirement. In this chapter, you learned about the different types of retirement vehicles available—from Roth IRAs and Traditional IRAs to 401(k)s and other options. You discovered how employer-sponsored plans can offer significant benefits, such as matching contributions and automatic escalations, which can dramatically boost your savings over time. Most importantly, you were guided on how to choose the right accounts based on your current tax situation, retirement income expectations, and personal goals.

Your journey toward early retirement and tax-free passive income depends on the decisions you make today. By understanding how each account works and leveraging the unique benefits they offer, you are putting yourself in a strong position to secure your future. Remember, every step you take in optimizing your savings strategy brings you closer to a life where you have control over your finances, free from the burden of excessive taxes. Use the information and strategies in this chapter to review your current plan, adjust your contributions, and confidently move toward a financially independent future.

As you continue to build your retirement portfolio, keep in mind that regular evaluations and adjustments are part of the process. Life changes, and so do your financial goals. Stay informed about tax laws and employer-sponsored benefits, and be ready to adapt your strategy as needed. With discipline, attention to detail, and a proactive approach, you can maximize the benefits of tax-advantaged accounts and create a stable, growing source of tax-free income for your retirement.

By taking full advantage of these accounts, you are not just saving money; you are making a long-term investment in your future. Every dollar you contribute is a building block toward the financial freedom you seek. Use the tools available to you wisely, and remember that each decision plays a vital role in shaping your retirement. Your commitment to learning and adapting your strategy will serve you well as you work toward the goal of early retirement with minimal tax liabilities.

Now is the time to take action. Review your current savings plan, explore any additional options available through your employer, and consider how a mix of different tax-advantaged accounts can help you achieve your financial goals. Your future self will thank you for the diligence and care you put into planning today. Stay focused, stay informed, and let each informed choice guide you toward a secure, tax-free retirement.

Chapter 4

Smart Saving & Budgeting Strategies

This chapter is dedicated to helping you take control of your finances by adopting smart saving and budgeting techniques that accelerate your journey toward early retirement and tax-free passive income. In these pages, you will learn how to manage your expenses effectively, use automation tools to save consistently, and strike a healthy balance between enjoying your life today and preparing for a secure tomorrow.

The methods presented here are rooted in practical experience and are designed to empower you with strategies that work in real life. As you read through this chapter, you will find relatable stories and actionable advice that remind you that every smart financial decision you make builds a foundation for the freedom you seek.

Expense Management for Accelerated Savings

When you set out to achieve financial independence, managing your expenses becomes one of the most critical steps on your path. You might feel overwhelmed when you see your monthly bills and daily spending add up, but learning to control your outgoings is a skill that you can develop with practice and discipline.

I remember a time when I would come home at the end of the day feeling defeated by the number of small expenses that had crept into my budget. A daily cup of coffee, a quick lunch out, and even a few spontaneous online purchases would gradually erode the funds I intended to save. It wasn't until I began tracking every dollar that I realized how much money was slipping away unnoticed.

You can start by listing your fixed expenses—rent, utilities, insurance, and loan payments—and then break down your variable expenses, like groceries, dining, entertainment, and transportation. This simple exercise opens your eyes to where you might trim unnecessary spending.

One effective technique is the "zero-based budget." With this method, you assign every dollar of your income a specific role before the month begins. Whether it's allocated toward a bill, a savings account, or even a small treat, every dollar has a destination. I recall the sense of relief I experienced when I first adopted a zero-based budget; I was no longer wondering where my money had gone at the end of the month. You too can feel that reassurance when you know that each dollar is working toward your goals. The process requires you to be honest about your spending habits.

It may be uncomfortable at first to see that you have been spending more on non-essential items than you thought, but this awareness is the first step toward meaningful change.

Another strategy is the use of the "50/30/20" rule, where 50% of your income goes to necessities, 30% to discretionary expenses, and 20% to savings and debt repayment. Although this rule is a guideline rather than a strict mandate, it can help you gauge whether your spending aligns with your long-term objectives. I remember tweaking my own percentages as I realized that I needed to boost my savings rate to reach my retirement goals faster. The key is to adjust the numbers in a way that works for you while keeping your primary objective in sight—accelerated savings for early retirement.

You might find that tracking your expenses digitally makes the process easier. Using spreadsheets or budgeting apps can help you monitor your spending in real time and quickly spot any discrepancies. I once started using an app that categorizes every transaction automatically. Soon, I was able to identify recurring expenses I hadn't even noticed—subscriptions I rarely used or dining expenses that were higher than expected. With this knowledge, I canceled or reduced several services, which freed up extra cash that I redirected toward my savings goals. These small changes add up over time, creating a significant boost to your savings.

In addition to tracking expenses, it is important to challenge yourself to cut down on wasteful spending. Look at your routine purchases and ask if each one truly contributes to your quality of life. Perhaps you can brew your coffee at home instead of buying it daily, or you might opt for cooking meals instead of ordering takeout frequently. I recall the difference in my bank balance after I made a deliberate choice to replace expensive habits with more cost-effective alternatives. The money saved in these everyday decisions can then be invested in your future, compounding over the years to create a sizable nest egg.

Being proactive with expense management means that you regularly review your budget and adjust your spending categories as your income and priorities change. Life is dynamic, and what works for you this year may need to be revised next year. I make it a habit to review my budget quarterly, noting where I have succeeded in reducing costs and where I might still be overspending. You should also set short-term savings targets and celebrate each time you meet them. Recognizing your progress reinforces positive behavior and keeps you motivated.

Effective expense management is not about depriving yourself of enjoyment—it is about making intentional choices. While you might cut back on certain luxuries, you should also allow room for activities that enrich your life. For instance, if you enjoy reading, you might switch from buying new books to borrowing from the library or using affordable digital subscriptions. It's all about striking a balance that aligns with your financial goals. By reducing waste and prioritizing essential expenses, you create room for accelerated savings, ensuring that more of your income contributes directly to your future freedom.

Remember, every dollar you save today is a building block for a better tomorrow. Even if the savings seem modest at first, the compound effect over years can be substantial. With each expense you eliminate, you are one step closer to achieving the tax-free retirement you dream about. Expense management is the cornerstone of a disciplined financial plan, and your commitment to this practice will serve you well as you build your wealth.

Automating Savings: Systems and Tools

One of the smartest moves you can make in your financial journey is to set up systems that automate your savings. When saving becomes automatic, you remove the temptation to spend extra cash and create a routine that steadily builds your retirement fund. Automation takes the guesswork out of saving and helps you stay on track, even when life gets busy.

I vividly remember the day I first set up an automatic transfer from my checking account to my savings account. It was a simple process, yet it felt like a turning point. Instead of manually transferring money each month, I arranged for a fixed amount to be sent automatically right after payday. This system ensured that I paid myself first, before any other expenses could claim a portion of my income. You too can experience the peace of mind that comes from knowing your savings are growing without requiring constant attention.

Many banks and financial institutions offer features that allow you to schedule transfers and even round-up transactions. For example, some services round up each purchase to the nearest dollar and transfer the difference to your savings account. I once set up such a system and was surprised to see how quickly those small amounts accumulated. Over time, the little amounts add up, and before you know it, you have a healthy cushion in your savings. These automated tools are designed to work in the background, making it easier for you to build wealth without disrupting your daily routine.

There are several budgeting and saving apps available that can help you manage your finances with minimal effort. Apps like Mint, YNAB (You Need A Budget), and Personal Capital provide you with insights into your spending habits, help you set goals, and even send reminders when it's time to save or pay bills. I experimented with a few different apps before settling on one that matched my style. The app not only tracked my expenses but also offered personalized tips on how to optimize my spending. When you use technology to support your financial goals, you create an environment where smart decisions are the easiest decisions to make.

Another tool that I found particularly helpful was an automated investment platform. These platforms, sometimes known as robo-advisors, allow you to invest your savings in a diversified portfolio that is managed with minimal input from you. Once set up, these services take care of asset allocation and rebalancing, ensuring that your investments stay aligned with your risk tolerance and long-term goals. I recall the relief of not having to worry about constantly monitoring market fluctuations—my robo-advisor handled the details, leaving me free to focus on other aspects of my life. With automation in place, you can make saving and investing almost effortless.

It is also wise to use calendar reminders and alerts to keep you informed about your financial progress. Many banks allow you to set up alerts for account balances, upcoming bill payments, or large transactions. These reminders help you avoid late fees and prevent unnecessary spending, keeping your savings plan on track. In my early days of budgeting, I missed a few due dates because I wasn't paying attention. Once I activated alerts on my phone, I rarely had issues with late payments. You can use similar tools to ensure that you always meet your financial commitments, which in turn supports your long-term saving goals.

Automating your savings not only helps you stay disciplined but also reduces the stress associated with managing money manually. There is a profound relief in knowing that the systems you have put in place are working for you around the clock. When saving is automated, you eliminate the risk of procrastination or the temptation to spend extra cash that could be better invested in your future. The less you have to think about saving, the more likely you are to stick with your plan over the long haul.

For those who are new to the idea of automation, start small. You might begin by setting up one automatic transfer per month and then gradually increase the frequency as you become more comfortable with the system. It is important to monitor the performance of these systems periodically, ensuring that the amounts and frequency still align with your financial goals. As your income grows or your expenses change, adjust your automated transfers accordingly. This proactive management ensures that your automated savings continue to serve you well as you work toward early retirement.

Using technology to automate your savings is a powerful strategy that can free up mental energy and reduce financial stress. With reliable systems in place, you allow your money to work quietly in the background, steadily moving you closer to your desired future. Every automated deposit, every small round-up, and every scheduled transfer is a step toward building a robust retirement fund without requiring constant effort on your part. As you embrace these tools, you create a disciplined environment that supports your overall financial well-being.

Balancing Lifestyle and Long-Term Goals

Striking the right balance between enjoying your life today and securing your future is an ongoing challenge. You may sometimes feel torn between spending on experiences and ensuring that your savings rate remains high. The key to overcoming this challenge is to develop a mindset that values both living well in the present and preparing for the future.

I recall a period in my life when I felt guilty about spending money on leisure activities, even though I had diligently set aside funds for retirement. I believed that every dollar spent on entertainment was a dollar that could have been saved. Over time, I learned that a balanced approach yields the best results. It is possible to enjoy your life now while still being committed to long-term financial goals. You must recognize that the purpose of saving is not to restrict your life entirely, but to empower you to make choices that lead to freedom later on.

One effective method for balancing these priorities is to allocate a specific portion of your income to both savings and discretionary spending. For instance, you might decide that 70% of your income goes toward essential expenses and savings, while the remaining 30% is earmarked for personal enjoyment. I adjusted my budget in this way after realizing that complete austerity was neither sustainable nor enjoyable.

When you give yourself permission to spend within limits, you are less likely to feel deprived, and you remain motivated to continue saving. This approach transforms budgeting from a burdensome chore into a practical tool that supports your overall happiness.

Another technique is to set clear short-term and long-term goals. Your long-term goal might be early retirement with a tax-free income, while your short-term goals could include saving for a vacation or a special purchase that enriches your life. I once set a goal to take a modest trip each year, even during times when I was focused on aggressive savings. These smaller goals provided periodic rewards that kept my motivation high without derailing my broader financial plan.

You can adopt a similar strategy by planning regular rewards that are funded by the savings you accumulate. This method helps maintain a positive relationship with money, ensuring that you enjoy the fruits of your labor without sacrificing your future.

It is also important to reassess your priorities periodically. As your life evolves, so do your needs and desires. The balance that works for you in your thirties might need adjustment in your forties or fifties. I have reexamined my spending and saving ratios at different stages of my career, and each time, I made small adjustments to ensure that my lifestyle and long-term objectives stayed in harmony. You might find it useful to set aside time each year to review your goals and adjust your budget accordingly. This practice keeps your financial plan dynamic and aligned with your current circumstances.

In addition to budgeting, you can explore ways to reduce costs without sacrificing quality of life. For example, instead of dining at expensive restaurants every weekend, you might host potlucks with friends or try cooking new recipes at home. I once joined a cooking club where members shared meals and recipes, which not only lowered my dining expenses but also enriched my social life. These creative solutions allow you to enjoy life while keeping expenses in check. When you discover new ways to cut costs in areas that do not diminish your overall satisfaction, you build extra savings that further support your long-term objectives.

Maintaining a balanced approach means that you are also mindful of your health and well-being. Physical and mental wellness contribute significantly to your quality of life, and investing in yourself should be part of your financial plan.

I learned that setting aside funds for exercise, hobbies, and personal development is not an indulgence but a necessary component of a well-rounded life. When you feel healthy and motivated, you are better equipped to pursue both your short-term pleasures and long-term financial goals. You can treat your budget as a flexible plan that adjusts to support your well-being, ensuring that you enjoy each phase of life without compromise.

Finally, remember that balance is not a one-time achievement but an ongoing process. Life will bring changes, unexpected expenses, and new opportunities, and your approach to spending and saving should evolve accordingly. The goal is to create a system that allows you to relish your present experiences while steadily building the future you desire. When you successfully balance your lifestyle and long-term goals, you achieve a sense of control and satisfaction that few financial plans can offer.

Each time you make a decision that honors both your immediate needs and your future dreams, you reinforce the habit of thoughtful spending and saving.

In this chapter, you have learned that smart saving and budgeting strategies are essential tools for accelerating your journey to early retirement and tax-free income. Effective expense management, the implementation of automated savings systems, and the delicate balance between enjoying your life today and planning for tomorrow are not mutually exclusive—they work best together. By tracking your expenses rigorously, using technology to automate your savings, and allocating funds wisely between your present needs and future goals, you create a financial system that supports your ambitions without sacrificing your quality of life.

Every step you take toward improving your budget and saving habits strengthens the foundation of your financial future. As you apply the strategies discussed here, remember that your financial choices today are investments in a tomorrow where you have the freedom to live on your own terms.

With discipline, thoughtful planning, and a commitment to balance, you will build the momentum necessary to achieve a secure and tax-efficient retirement. Your journey is marked by small, consistent actions that, over time, yield significant rewards. Stay focused on your priorities, celebrate your progress along the way, and remain open to refining your approach as your circumstances evolve.

Your financial future is built one decision at a time. Embrace the challenge of managing your expenses, harness the power of automated tools, and enjoy the process of striking the right balance between living well now and saving for the future. The freedom you seek is within reach when you commit to smart saving and budgeting strategies that empower you every day. Let your choices be a reflection of both your values and your long-term aspirations, and remember that each mindful decision brings you closer to the secure, tax-free retirement you deserve.

Chapter 5

Investment Strategies for Passive Income

This chapter is devoted to showing you how to build a steady stream of passive income that can support an early, tax-free retirement. Here, you will learn about three key areas: dividend stocks, ETFs, and index funds; real estate through rental properties and REITs; and alternative income sources. Each section is filled with practical advice, real-life examples, and clear strategies that you can use to make your money work harder for you. By using these investment strategies, you create a reliable income stream that supports your long-term goal of financial independence.

Dividend Stocks, ETFs, and Index Funds

Investing in dividend stocks, ETFs, and index funds is a popular way to generate passive income while building wealth over time. These investments provide returns through periodic dividend payouts and the appreciation of your capital. When you invest in dividend stocks, you are purchasing shares in companies that share a portion of their profits with you on a regular basis. I remember when I first started investing, I chose companies with a long history of paying consistent dividends. The steady cash flow I received gave me confidence that I was on the right track. You, too, can enjoy that sense of security by choosing investments that generate reliable income.

Dividend stocks often come from established companies in industries such as utilities, consumer goods, and healthcare. These companies typically have stable earnings and a record of paying dividends even during challenging economic times. For you, these stocks can serve as a cornerstone of your investment portfolio. They not only provide income but also tend to show less volatility compared to growth stocks. Over time, as you reinvest the dividends, your returns can grow through the power of compounding. This strategy enables you to build wealth passively and helps you reach your retirement goals sooner.

ETFs (Exchange-Traded Funds) and index funds are another excellent way to create a diversified investment portfolio. These funds pool money from many investors to buy a broad selection of stocks, bonds, or other assets. Because they track market indices, such as the S&P 500, ETFs and index funds typically have lower fees compared to actively managed funds.

I recall the moment I shifted some of my assets into a low-cost index fund. Not only did I enjoy the benefits of diversification, but I also found that my overall investment performance improved without the need for constant monitoring. You have the option to choose from a wide variety of ETFs and index funds that match your risk tolerance and financial goals.

The benefits of dividend stocks, ETFs, and index funds extend beyond the dividends themselves. They help you avoid the burden of high fees and reduce the need for frequent trading, which can incur additional costs. When you receive a dividend payment, you have the choice to reinvest it or use it to meet other financial needs.

Reinvesting dividends is a proven method to accelerate the growth of your portfolio. I remember setting up an automatic dividend reinvestment plan (DRIP) and being amazed at how quickly my portfolio grew over time. Each dividend payment was reinvested, leading to the purchase of additional shares and, in turn, generating even more dividends. You too can set up DRIPs with many brokerage accounts, ensuring that your money is continuously working to generate further income.

One of the key advantages of these investments is that they are relatively simple to manage. With dividend stocks and index funds, you can set up a long-term strategy that requires minimal daily attention. This allows you to focus on other aspects of your life while your investments do the heavy lifting. I remember the peace of mind that came with knowing that my portfolio was designed to provide passive income without requiring constant adjustments. For you, the ability to invest and let your money grow on its own is a major step toward achieving a tax-free retirement.

When you invest in dividend stocks and funds, it's important to keep an eye on the payout ratios, dividend growth rates, and the overall health of the companies or funds in which you invest. Look for those that have a strong track record and stable earnings.

Over time, as you receive dividend payments, you might choose to reinvest them or use them to pay down debt. This flexibility helps you maintain control over your financial future. In my own experience, I have found that a blend of dividend-paying stocks and broad-market index funds provides both stability and growth potential. This approach can work well for you, especially if you are focused on generating income without taking on too much risk.

As you build your portfolio with these assets, remember that diversification is key. By spreading your investments across different sectors and asset classes, you reduce the risk that a downturn in one area will significantly affect your overall returns. You might allocate a portion of your portfolio to high-dividend stocks, another portion to growth-oriented index funds, and even a small part to sector-specific ETFs that align with your interests.

The right mix will depend on your individual goals and risk tolerance. I recall revising my allocation several times as my financial goals evolved; each change helped me better manage risk and improve returns. For you, maintaining a diversified portfolio means that you can adjust your strategy as market conditions change without jeopardizing your overall plan.

Finally, tax efficiency plays a critical role in your long-term success. Investments in dividend stocks, ETFs, and index funds can be held in tax-advantaged accounts, where your dividends may grow either tax-free or tax-deferred. Placing these assets in a Roth IRA or a Traditional IRA can help minimize the tax drag on your returns. I learned early in my investment journey that paying taxes on your gains can significantly reduce the compound growth of your portfolio.

By using tax-advantaged accounts, you ensure that more of your money is reinvested for the future. You have the power to structure your investments in a way that reduces your tax liabilities and speeds up your journey to a secure, tax-free retirement.

Real Estate: Rental Properties and REITs

Investing in real estate offers another path to generating passive income. You can choose to purchase rental properties or invest in Real Estate Investment Trusts (REITs), both of which can provide steady cash flow and long-term capital appreciation. Real estate investments have a tangible quality that many investors find appealing because they involve physical assets that can offer protection against inflation.

When you purchase a rental property, you become a landlord, earning monthly income from tenants. I recall the excitement I felt when I acquired my first rental property. The idea of receiving regular rent checks provided a tangible sense of progress toward my financial goals.

Owning a rental property can be both a source of income and an investment that appreciates over time. Rental properties can be especially attractive if you select locations with strong demand for housing, where rental rates tend to increase over time. As the property appreciates, you benefit from capital gains, while the rental income helps cover any mortgage payments and maintenance costs.

Managing rental properties requires active involvement, especially in the early stages. You may need to handle tenant screening, repairs, and occasional disputes. I remember the first time I had to resolve an issue with a tenant—it was challenging, but it taught me valuable lessons about property management and the importance of proper planning. Over time, you might decide to hire a property management company to handle day-to-day operations, which allows you to focus on your other investments.

The key is to start with properties that match your expertise and risk tolerance. For you, if you are willing to take on the responsibilities of a landlord, rental properties can generate significant passive income. They also offer tax advantages, such as deductions for mortgage interest, property taxes, and depreciation. These tax benefits help you keep more of your rental income and further accelerate your progress toward financial freedom.

If you prefer a more hands-off approach, REITs provide a convenient alternative to direct real estate investment. REITs are companies that own, operate, or finance income-producing real estate. By investing in REITs, you can gain exposure to a diversified portfolio of properties without having to manage them yourself.

I remember reading about how REITs work and feeling intrigued by the idea of owning a share in a portfolio of office buildings, shopping centers, or apartment complexes. For you, REITs can offer regular dividend payments, as most are required by law to distribute a large percentage of their income to shareholders. This income stream can be an excellent supplement to your overall investment strategy.

REITs are traded on stock exchanges, which means you can buy and sell them just like any other stock. This liquidity makes them a flexible option if you need access to cash or want to adjust your portfolio quickly. I once shifted part of my portfolio into a REIT-focused ETF, which provided me with both diversification and a steady income stream. You have the advantage of accessing the real estate market without the commitment of managing physical properties.

Additionally, many REITs offer the potential for capital appreciation, meaning that as the underlying properties improve or the market strengthens, the value of your investment can grow. The dividends you receive from REITs are often higher than those from traditional stocks, making them an attractive option for building passive income.

Whether you choose rental properties or REITs, real estate investments offer the possibility of both income and growth. Rental properties provide the satisfaction of owning a physical asset and the opportunity to generate monthly cash flow, while REITs offer the benefits of diversification, liquidity, and professional management.

The decision may come down to how much time you want to invest in managing your assets. If you are hands-on and enjoy working with properties, rental investments might be the right choice. On the other hand, if you prefer a more passive approach, REITs allow you to invest in real estate without the responsibilities of property management.

Another important aspect of real estate investing is understanding the local market conditions. When you purchase a rental property, factors such as job growth, population trends, and local amenities can influence the demand for housing and the potential for rent increases. I learned this lesson the hard way when I bought a property in an area that later experienced a decline in demand. For you, conducting thorough research before investing is crucial.

Look for markets with a strong economic base and a history of steady rent growth. These factors can help ensure that your investment remains robust even during economic fluctuations.

Financing is also a key element when investing in real estate. Many investors use mortgages to purchase properties, which allows you to leverage your investment and control a larger asset with a smaller initial outlay. However, using debt wisely is important. I once overextended myself by taking on too much debt, which put a strain on my cash flow during a period of low occupancy.

You must be mindful of your leverage and ensure that your rental income can comfortably cover your mortgage payments, maintenance, and other expenses. Keeping a close eye on your debt levels will help you avoid financial stress and maintain a steady income stream.

Tax benefits in real estate are another compelling reason to add these investments to your portfolio. You can deduct mortgage interest, property taxes, and even a portion of your operating expenses. In addition, depreciation can significantly reduce your taxable income, even if your property is appreciating in value. I experienced firsthand how these deductions made a real difference in my annual tax bill, leaving me with more capital to reinvest. For you, these tax advantages can improve the overall returns on your investment and contribute to your goal of a tax-free retirement.

Exploring Alternative Income Sources

Beyond traditional investments in stocks and real estate, there are numerous alternative income sources that can enhance your passive income strategy. These sources offer flexibility and the potential for high returns if you are willing to learn and take a strategic approach.

One popular alternative is investing in peer-to-peer lending platforms. By lending money directly to individuals or small businesses through online platforms, you can earn interest rates that often surpass those of conventional savings accounts. I remember the first time I tried peer-to-peer lending; I was both excited and cautious. The platform provided detailed information about borrowers, and as I built a diversified portfolio of loans, I was pleased to see steady returns.

Peer-to-peer lending can serve as a useful supplement to more traditional investments. It allows you to generate income on a regular basis while spreading risk across many small loans. Always research the platforms thoroughly, as different services come with varying levels of risk and return. With careful selection, you can enjoy a reliable income stream from these alternative loans.

Another option to explore is creating digital products or licensing your expertise. If you have skills or knowledge in a particular area, you might develop online courses, eBooks, or software that can generate royalties over time. I once worked with a mentor who had turned his professional experience into a series of online courses that consistently earned passive income. You have the chance to leverage your personal expertise and interests to create products that provide value to others while earning money for you. Digital products have low overhead costs and can be scaled easily, meaning that once you create the product, it has the potential to generate revenue indefinitely with minimal additional effort.

Investing in small businesses or startups can also be an attractive option for generating alternative income. Through crowdfunding platforms or angel investing, you can support emerging companies in exchange for a share of their profits. I recall hearing about a friend who invested in a startup that eventually became successful, yielding a significant return on his investment.

For you, this form of investment comes with higher risk but also the potential for high rewards. It is essential to perform thorough due diligence and understand that not every investment will turn out as planned. However, if you spread your investments across multiple ventures, you can mitigate some of the risks while still enjoying the possibility of lucrative returns.

Royalties from intellectual property, such as patents, music, or writing, are another source of alternative income. If you have a creative side or have developed an innovative idea, licensing your work to companies can provide you with regular royalty payments. I once met an entrepreneur who held a patent for a small device that, once licensed to a manufacturer, generated a steady stream of income. For you, finding ways to monetize your ideas can be a powerful addition to your passive income strategy.

These income streams are often highly scalable and have the potential to continue growing over time without significant additional work.

Finally, you might explore investments in commodities, cryptocurrencies, or even art and collectibles. These asset classes can offer diversification and the potential for strong returns, though they often come with higher volatility. I have seen both the highs and lows of alternative investments, and I learned that maintaining a balanced portfolio is key. For you, if you choose to invest in these areas, start small and only allocate a portion of your portfolio to these assets. This way, you can experiment and learn without exposing your overall financial plan to excessive risk.

One important lesson that I have learned from exploring alternative income sources is the value of flexibility. The world of investments is full of opportunities that might not fit into traditional categories. By remaining open to new ideas and being willing to research and experiment, you can discover income streams that align with your strengths and interests.

The willingness to explore these alternatives can significantly supplement your primary investment strategy, increasing the overall stability of your income while pushing you closer to your goal of financial independence.

As you assess these alternative income sources, focus on those that complement your existing investments. Think about how each additional income stream can work together to create a more robust financial picture. You might start with one or two alternatives, and over time, expand your portfolio as you gain experience and confidence.

The key is to stay informed, be disciplined about risk management, and keep your long-term objectives in mind. When you incorporate a mix of traditional and alternative investments, you build a more resilient portfolio that can withstand market fluctuations and other uncertainties.

Investment strategies for passive income are a vital component of achieving an early, tax-free retirement. In this chapter, you learned about three main approaches: building a portfolio of dividend stocks, ETFs, and index funds; investing in real estate through rental properties and REITs; and exploring alternative income sources such as peer-to-peer lending, digital products, small business investments, and royalties. Each of these strategies offers its own set of advantages and risks, but all share one common goal: to generate reliable income that requires little day-to-day effort.

As you work to create a diversified portfolio, you empower yourself to build wealth steadily over time. Whether you choose to reinvest your dividends, manage rental properties, or use technology to automate income from digital products, every decision you make moves you closer to a future where your money works for you. I have seen firsthand how smart, informed investment choices can transform financial prospects. You, too, can enjoy the benefits of a well-structured passive income strategy that supports both your current lifestyle and your long-term goals.

Keep in mind that successful investing is not about finding a single magic formula but about consistently applying sound strategies, reviewing your progress, and adjusting your approach as needed. By combining traditional investments with alternative income sources, you create a safety net that protects your finances against market volatility and unexpected expenses. Every dividend received, every rent check collected, and every royalty payment adds to your momentum, moving you steadily toward the independence you desire.

Your journey toward a tax-free retirement through passive income begins with these informed choices. Stay disciplined, continue learning, and remember that every investment decision is a step toward a future where you are free to live on your own terms. With persistence and smart planning, the passive income strategies in this chapter will help you build a stable, diversified portfolio that supports your financial goals for years to come.

Chapter 6

Tax-Free Investment Vehicles

In this chapter, you will learn about strategies that help you build a tax-efficient investment portfolio to support early retirement and tax-free passive income. The focus here is on investment tools that minimize your tax liability while growing your wealth steadily. You will explore municipal bonds and tax-exempt securities, use of life insurance and annuities, and methods to structure your investments for optimal tax efficiency.

I recall the first time I encountered these vehicles. The complexity of tax laws was daunting, but as I studied and applied these strategies, I realized that smart planning could significantly reduce the taxes on my investment returns. That discovery changed my financial outlook—and it can change yours too. With the right knowledge, you can design a portfolio that works in your favor, allowing you to keep more of your hard-earned money.

Municipal bonds offer interest income that is free from federal, and often state, taxes. Life insurance and annuities can provide additional benefits by sheltering growth from immediate taxation. Furthermore, by arranging your investments with care, you can reduce taxable events and boost long-term returns.

This chapter provides practical insights, supported by personal experiences, to help you understand each tax-free vehicle and integrate it into your overall strategy. The guidance here is straightforward and designed to empower you to make informed decisions that align with your financial goals.

As you read, reflect on your current investment strategy and assess how tax efficiency might enhance your progress toward a secure, independent future. Your financial journey is built on the choices you make today, and this chapter is here to equip you with the knowledge needed to reduce your tax burden and achieve lasting financial freedom. By using these strategies wisely, you lay a strong foundation for a prosperous retirement journey ahead.

Municipal Bonds and Tax-Exempt Securities

Municipal bonds are debt securities issued by state, city, or local governments to finance public projects. When you invest in municipal bonds, you lend money to the issuer in exchange for periodic interest payments and the return of principal at maturity. One of the key benefits of these bonds is that their interest income is typically exempt from federal income taxes—and in many cases, state and local taxes as well. This tax exemption makes municipal bonds an attractive option for investors seeking to maximize after-tax returns.

I remember the first time I invested in a municipal bond; I was impressed by the dual advantage of steady income and the tax relief it provided, which allowed me to keep more of my earnings.

Municipal bonds come in two main types: general obligation bonds and revenue bonds. General obligation bonds are backed by the full credit and taxing power of the issuing government, often making them a safer investment. Revenue bonds, on the other hand, are secured by specific revenue streams from projects such as toll roads, utilities, or airports.

While revenue bonds may offer higher yields, they also carry additional risks related to the performance of the underlying project. For you, understanding the distinctions between these bond types is critical when evaluating your risk tolerance and investment goals.

Beyond individual bonds, tax-exempt securities can include other instruments designed to reduce your tax liability. Certain government-issued securities and specially structured funds provide income that is shielded from taxation, thereby increasing your net yield. I once rebalanced my portfolio to include a mix of individual municipal bonds and municipal bond funds, and the boost to my after-tax returns was significant. This experience taught me that strategic allocation to tax-free investments can have a profound impact on overall financial health.

It is also valuable to pay attention to credit ratings and maturity dates when selecting municipal bonds. Credit ratings reveal the issuer's ability to meet its obligations, while the maturity date tells you when you will receive your principal back. Generally, bonds with higher credit ratings offer lower yields because of their reduced risk, whereas bonds with lower ratings may provide higher returns but come with increased risk. I spent considerable time researching various bonds before making an investment, ensuring that the options I chose matched my long-term plan and risk appetite. For you, maintaining a balanced portfolio means weighing the trade-offs between yield and risk carefully.

Market conditions and interest rate trends further influence the performance of municipal bonds. In a rising interest rate environment, bond prices tend to decline, which can affect the value of your investments if you decide to sell before maturity.

However, if you hold your bonds until maturity, you are guaranteed to receive the interest payments and full principal amount. This stability is one of the main attractions of municipal bonds, especially for investors aiming for predictable income streams. I have experienced both market fluctuations and periods of steady growth with my municipal bond investments, and those experiences underscored the importance of a long-term perspective. For you, adopting patience and focusing on bonds held to maturity can help mitigate short-term market volatility.

Another useful concept is the tax-equivalent yield, which allows you to compare the yield of a tax-exempt bond with that of a taxable bond by adjusting for your tax rate. Calculating the tax-equivalent yield provides a clear numerical basis for decision-making and can reassure you that you are optimizing your portfolio effectively. I vividly recall calculating the tax-equivalent yield on a potential bond purchase and being pleasantly surprised at how favorable the numbers were.

Mastering this concept can enhance your ability to choose investments that best align with your financial goals.

Investing in municipal bond funds is another option to gain exposure to tax-exempt securities. These funds pool money from many investors to acquire a diversified portfolio of municipal bonds. The benefit of such funds is that they offer instant diversification and professional management—an attractive choice if you do not have the time or expertise to research individual bonds.

I transitioned a portion of my investments into a municipal bond fund and found that it simplified my portfolio management while still delivering attractive tax-free returns. A well-managed bond fund can provide both convenience and consistent performance, making it an essential component of your tax-free investment strategy.

Municipal bonds and other tax-exempt securities offer a reliable way to generate steady income while reducing the tax drag on your earnings. They serve as a stable foundation in your investment portfolio and can help you reach your retirement goals by preserving more of your returns. With careful selection, continuous monitoring, and a long-term perspective, these investments can significantly contribute to your journey toward a secure, tax-free retirement.

Utilizing Life Insurance and Annuities

Life insurance and annuities are financial instruments that can serve dual purposes: providing protection and offering a vehicle for tax-advantaged growth. These products, when used effectively, can become an integral part of your tax-free investment plan. Permanent life insurance policies, such as whole life or universal life, not only supply a death benefit but also accumulate cash value over time. This cash value grows tax-deferred, and you can access it through policy loans or withdrawals under favorable conditions. I remember the first time I learned that a permanent life insurance policy could serve as a supplemental retirement asset. It was eye-opening to see that the policy's cash value could be tapped for tax-free income in retirement, adding flexibility to my financial plan.

Annuities, by contrast, are contracts with insurance companies designed to provide a steady income stream, either immediately or later in life. There are various types of annuities—fixed annuities, which offer a guaranteed rate of return, and variable annuities, where the returns depend on the performance of underlying investments. Choosing between different annuity types depends on your risk tolerance and income needs.

I spent time evaluating several annuity products before selecting one that matched my long-term income requirements. The primary benefit of annuities is the ability to defer taxes on your earnings until you begin receiving payments, which can be advantageous if you expect to be in a lower tax bracket during retirement.

A strategy I found effective was to use a blend of life insurance and annuities to create a diversified income stream. By balancing the tax-deferred growth of a permanent life insurance policy with the predictable income from an annuity, you can reduce your reliance on taxable investments. This approach provided me with reassurance, knowing that I had multiple sources of income in retirement that were shielded from immediate taxation.

This diversification helps smooth out cash flow and offers a buffer against market volatility.

It is important to understand the cost structures and fees associated with these products. Permanent life insurance policies, for example, usually have higher premiums than term life insurance, and annuities often include management fees that can affect overall returns. I spent considerable time comparing different products and consulting with financial professionals to ensure I was getting true value. Being aware of these costs and understanding their impact on net returns is essential. Read all policy details carefully and ask about surrender charges, administrative fees, and any other costs that might affect your long-term outcomes.

Another critical aspect is the tax treatment of withdrawals. With a permanent life insurance policy, if you take out a loan against the cash value, the loan is generally tax-free as long as the policy remains active.

However, if the policy lapses or if withdrawals exceed the total premiums paid, you could incur a tax liability. Likewise, annuity payouts are taxed as ordinary income when received. It is crucial to plan your withdrawals carefully to maximize tax benefits. I restructured my annuity withdrawals to minimize the taxable portion of each payment, ensuring a steady and efficient income stream. For you, such careful planning can greatly enhance the benefits these products offer.

Furthermore, some advanced life insurance policies come with optional riders that can enhance benefits or add flexibility. Riders such as accelerated death benefits or long-term care provisions can address specific needs as you age.

I have witnessed policyholders use these options to manage unexpected expenses without disrupting their overall financial plan. For you, exploring additional features may provide extra security and adaptability as your needs evolve.

In summary, life insurance and annuities offer a unique blend of protection, growth, and income. When used strategically, they can help build a robust, tax-efficient foundation for retirement. By understanding the various products, comparing costs, and planning your withdrawals effectively, you can integrate these instruments into your overall investment strategy.

This integration not only reduces taxable income during your working years but also provides a dependable source of income when you retire. With careful planning and informed decision-making, you can harness the benefits of life insurance and annuities to support a secure, tax-free retirement.

Structuring Investments to Minimize Taxation

Structuring your investments to minimize taxation is a critical aspect of building a tax-free retirement portfolio. The goal is to arrange your assets so that you reduce the tax drag on your returns and keep more of your money working for you over time. One fundamental strategy is to place investments that generate significant taxable income in tax-advantaged accounts, such as IRAs or 401(k)s.

For example, if you hold bonds or dividend-paying stocks in a taxable account, the income they produce is subject to tax each year—reducing your overall yield. I recall revising my portfolio to move income-producing assets into a Roth IRA, where both growth and withdrawals are tax-free. That change dramatically improved my net returns and set me on the path toward a more efficient retirement strategy.

Another effective method is tax-loss harvesting, which involves selling investments that have declined in value to offset gains from other investments. This technique can lower your taxable income and is especially useful during volatile market periods. I worked with a financial advisor who identified opportunities for tax-loss harvesting during a market downturn. By realizing some losses and reinvesting the proceeds, I was able to reduce my tax bill without significantly altering my overall investment strategy. For you, mastering tax-loss harvesting requires regular portfolio reviews and a willingness to adjust your holdings when market conditions call for it.

Timing your transactions also plays a vital role in tax efficiency. Long-term capital gains, which apply to assets held for more than one year, are taxed at a lower rate than short-term gains. By holding investments longer, you can benefit from these reduced rates. I once resisted the urge to sell a stock after a quick gain, opting instead for a longer holding period and eventually enjoying a much lower tax rate on the profit. For you, adopting a long-term perspective can be one of the simplest yet most effective ways to reduce your tax burden over time.

Using tax-efficient mutual funds and ETFs is another important tactic. Many funds are managed to minimize taxable events, such as frequent trading or capital gains distributions. Index funds, for instance, typically generate fewer taxable events than actively managed funds because of their lower turnover rates. I shifted a portion of my portfolio into tax-efficient funds, and this move not only reduced my tax liability but also improved my overall returns. For you, selecting funds that emphasize tax efficiency can significantly boost your after-tax income.

Asset location is yet another key principle. This means placing different types of investments in the accounts that best suit their tax characteristics. For example, high-growth assets that generate significant capital gains might be best held in tax-deferred accounts, while tax-efficient assets like index funds can remain in taxable accounts. I learned that aligning an asset's tax profile with the right account can optimize overall performance. For you, careful asset location can lead to a more balanced and tax-efficient strategy over the long term.

Some investors also explore advanced structures such as charitable remainder trusts or private placement life insurance to further reduce tax liabilities. These specialized vehicles can offer significant tax benefits, though they require advanced planning and professional advice. I once consulted with a tax expert about using a charitable remainder trust to reduce estate taxes while providing an income stream. For you, these strategies may be worth exploring if your financial situation is complex and you have substantial assets to protect from high tax rates.

Finally, it is essential to review your investment portfolio regularly and adjust your strategy as tax laws and personal circumstances evolve. Tax policies change over time, and staying informed allows you to adapt your approach to maintain optimal tax efficiency.

I make it a habit to assess my portfolio annually, ensuring that my asset allocation and investment locations continue to align with my long-term goals. For you, regular reviews are a necessary part of any successful strategy, keeping your plan responsive and effective.

Ultimately, structuring your investments to minimize taxation is not a one-time decision but a continuous process of optimization. By strategically placing assets, employing techniques like tax-loss harvesting, and maintaining a long-term view, you can significantly reduce the tax burden on your returns. This enables you to accumulate wealth more efficiently and move closer to the financial independence you desire. With careful planning, ongoing monitoring, and a readiness to adjust your strategy as needed, you can build a portfolio that maximizes after-tax returns and supports a secure, tax-free retirement.

Chapter 7

Entrepreneurial Income & Side Hustles

This chapter focuses on expanding your financial opportunities through entrepreneurial income and side hustles. You will learn how to build additional revenue streams, make use of technology and automation, and review real examples of successful passive income models. This chapter is designed to provide you with actionable strategies and real-life stories that show how a proactive approach to earning extra income can lead to a more secure, tax-free retirement. Every step you take in diversifying your income sources is a step toward greater control over your financial future.

Creating Additional Revenue Streams

When you think about your income, you may realize that relying solely on your day job can limit your financial potential. By creating additional revenue streams, you open up the possibility of earning money from various sources, reducing your dependence on a single paycheck and accelerating your progress toward early retirement.

Expanding Beyond Your Main Job

You have skills, interests, and experiences that can generate extra income outside of your primary work. Many people start small by offering freelance services or selling items online, and these modest ventures can eventually grow into significant revenue sources. I remember the early days when

I spent evenings working on projects that allowed me to use my skills in writing and graphic design. What began as a small side project soon developed into a steady income stream that contributed to my savings goals. You have the power to transform your hobbies or expertise into money-making opportunities.

To start, identify the talents or passions that you can monetize. It might be consulting, tutoring, coaching, or even creating digital content. For example, if you have a knack for cooking, you could create a blog, start a YouTube channel, or even offer virtual cooking classes. I once met someone who turned his passion for woodworking into an online store that now supplies handcrafted furniture to customers around the country. You may find that your creative side can lead to unexpected income sources.

Building a Business on the Side

Developing a side business is one of the most effective ways to create additional revenue streams. This does not necessarily mean quitting your day job immediately; rather, it involves dedicating a portion of your free time to building a business that generates passive or semi-passive income. Many successful entrepreneurs began by working on their business ideas in the evenings or on weekends until they could see a consistent return. I recall working long nights while my regular job paid the bills, and over time, my side business started to pay dividends that I reinvested into my long-term goals.

When starting a side business, focus on solving a problem or meeting a need in the market. A practical approach is to choose a niche where you have expertise and where demand exists. Once you establish your business, even a modest profit can be reinvested to expand your operations or saved to boost your retirement fund. You can begin with a lean startup model—keeping costs low and reinvesting profits into growth. Many of the ideas that led to successful side hustles started with simple offerings and evolved as the market responded.

Diversifying Your Income Sources

As you build your extra revenue streams, it is important to maintain diversity. Relying on one side business or freelance gig might work for a while, but diversification protects you from changes in demand or market fluctuations. You might combine several smaller ventures rather than putting all your energy into a single project. For instance, you might run a small e-commerce site, offer online consulting, and create digital products, all at the same time. I once had a friend who managed to balance multiple side projects, and the diversity of his income streams helped him weather economic downturns without much stress. For you, a diversified approach means that if one revenue stream slows down, the others can still provide steady income.

A key part of diversifying is to continuously look for new opportunities. Monitor market trends, stay connected with communities in your areas of interest, and be willing to experiment with new ideas. You may find that what started as a small project evolves into something much larger. The extra income you generate is not only beneficial for your current lifestyle but also accelerates your ability to invest in tax-free retirement vehicles.

The Importance of Passive Income

Passive income is income that requires minimal daily effort to maintain once it is set up. This form of income is particularly valuable when you aim for early retirement, as it allows you to earn money even when you are not actively working. Some side hustles may demand initial hard work but can eventually turn into passive income sources.

For example, writing an eBook or creating an online course requires effort upfront, but once it is published, you may earn royalties or sales without continuous active management. I recall spending months developing an online course that eventually became a steady source of income, freeing up my time while still contributing to my savings. For you, creating products or systems that generate passive income is a powerful way to reach financial freedom.

When you set up passive income streams, you benefit from the opportunity to work on your own schedule. You are no longer tied to the clock, which means you can spend more time on activities that matter to you while still receiving a consistent cash flow. The key is to invest time in building these systems so that they continue to work in the background. Whether it is setting up an affiliate website, developing a mobile app, or licensing your work, the idea is to create an asset that pays you over time. The income from these ventures can then be reinvested, helping to accelerate your path toward a tax-free retirement.

Mindset for Entrepreneurial Success

Developing additional revenue streams requires a mindset of persistence and continuous learning. You will face challenges along the way—mistakes, setbacks, and moments of doubt are natural parts of any entrepreneurial journey. I have experienced failures and learned from them, each misstep teaching me valuable lessons that improved my approach. Embracing these challenges as learning opportunities is essential. Stay curious, be open to feedback, and adjust your strategies as needed.

It is also important to set realistic goals and track your progress. Define clear benchmarks for what you want to achieve with each revenue stream and monitor your performance over time. Celebrate your successes, even if they seem small, and use setbacks as motivation to work harder. Keeping a journal or a progress tracker can help you remain focused on your objectives. Every new revenue stream you develop is a step toward financial independence and early retirement. With commitment and smart planning, the extra income you generate will compound, significantly boosting your overall savings.

Action Steps for Creating Revenue Streams

1. **Identify Your Strengths:** List your skills, hobbies, and interests that have potential market value.

2. **Research Opportunities:** Look into markets where your talents can fill a need. Use online resources and community feedback.

3. **Start Small:** Launch a pilot project or a small side gig. Test the market and gather feedback.

4. **Invest Time Wisely:** Dedicate specific hours each week to your side hustle. Treat it like a part-time business.

5. **Reinvest Profits:** Use the additional income to improve your operations, expand your offerings, or boost your savings.

6. **Review and Diversify:** Regularly assess your revenue streams and add new ones as opportunities arise.

By following these steps, you can create additional revenue streams that contribute to your financial goals without overwhelming your daily life. Your extra income will not only support your current lifestyle but also help you invest more aggressively in tax-free accounts, ultimately moving you closer to the retirement you desire.

Leveraging Technology and Automation

In today's fast-paced world, technology plays a crucial role in maximizing efficiency and scaling your income. Using automation tools can simplify many aspects of your side hustles and entrepreneurial ventures, allowing you to focus on strategy and growth instead of routine tasks.

Embracing Digital Tools

Digital tools have transformed the way people manage their finances and run businesses. You can use software to track expenses, manage customer relationships, schedule social media posts, and even handle transactions automatically. I remember the relief I felt when I started using a customer relationship management tool to handle inquiries from my online store. What used to take hours of manual work was reduced to a few clicks, freeing up time for other important tasks. Leveraging digital tools means you can streamline operations and scale your business faster without sacrificing quality.

There are many platforms available that can help you manage various aspects of your business. For example, accounting software like QuickBooks or FreshBooks automates bookkeeping tasks, reducing errors and saving time. Similarly, project management tools such as Trello or Asana help you organize tasks and collaborate with team members efficiently.

If you are selling products online, e-commerce platforms like Shopify or WooCommerce offer integrated solutions for inventory management, order processing, and payment handling. These tools are designed to make your workload lighter and allow you to concentrate on growth. By embracing technology, you ensure that the systems you build are efficient, accurate, and scalable.

Automating Routine Tasks

Automation is about setting up systems that run with minimal intervention. For many side hustles, the repetitive tasks can consume valuable time. By automating these processes, you can ensure consistency and free yourself to focus on higher-level strategies. I recall spending countless hours manually processing orders until I implemented an automated system that handled everything from inventory updates to customer notifications. The change was dramatic, and the extra time I gained allowed me to explore new business opportunities. For you, automation is a tool that not only improves efficiency but also enhances the quality of your services.

Email marketing is another area where automation can have a big impact. Using platforms like Mailchimp or ConvertKit, you can set up automated campaigns that nurture leads and keep customers engaged without constant oversight. Once these systems are in place, they work around the clock, sending out newsletters, promotional offers, and follow-up messages.

This not only saves you time but also creates a consistent revenue stream by keeping your audience informed and connected. I once set up an automated email sequence for my digital products, and the steady flow of communication boosted my sales significantly. For you, automating email marketing can help maintain customer relationships and drive sales even when you are not actively working on it.

Social media scheduling tools are equally valuable. Platforms such as Hootsuite or Buffer allow you to plan and schedule posts in advance, ensuring that your social media presence remains active without daily effort. These tools free you from the constant pressure to post content and let you focus on developing quality material that engages your audience. I experienced a boost in online engagement after switching to a scheduled posting routine, and this change allowed me to maintain an active online presence effortlessly. For you, using scheduling tools ensures that you maintain momentum and consistency, which is key to building a loyal following.

Outsourcing and Virtual Assistance

Another important aspect of leveraging technology is the ability to outsource tasks that do not require your personal touch. The gig economy has grown significantly, and you can now hire virtual assistants, freelancers, or specialized service providers to handle aspects of your business. I once hired a virtual assistant to manage customer support for my online ventures. The extra help allowed me to focus on strategy and business development rather than routine tasks. Outsourcing can be a game-changer, allowing you to scale operations while keeping overhead costs low.

Freelance platforms such as Upwork, Fiverr, and Freelancer offer access to professionals with skills ranging from graphic design to web development and content creation. If you find that certain tasks are taking too much of your time, delegate them to experts who can handle the work efficiently. This way, you maintain quality without overburdening yourself. In my experience, outsourcing tasks like social media management or blog writing has allowed me to expand my business without compromising on quality. For you, finding reliable partners can significantly boost your productivity and open up new opportunities for revenue growth.

Integrating Systems for Seamless Operations

The key to successful automation and technology use is integration. When your various systems work together seamlessly, you create an ecosystem that operates smoothly without requiring constant manual intervention. For example, you might integrate your e-commerce platform with your accounting software and email marketing tool so that every sale is automatically recorded, and follow-up emails are sent to customers. I once set up a fully integrated system for my online business, and the efficiency gains were remarkable. This kind of integration means that you can run multiple revenue streams simultaneously without becoming overwhelmed by administrative tasks.

Investing time in setting up these systems can yield long-term benefits. It might take an initial investment of time and resources, but the payoff is substantial. Once your systems are in place, they operate in the background, allowing you to focus on strategic decisions and growth initiatives. You will find that the automation of routine tasks not only saves time but also reduces errors and improves overall business performance. Every minute saved through automation is a minute you can spend on activities that truly move your business forward.

Measuring and Optimizing Performance

Technology and automation are only as effective as the results they produce. It is important for you to regularly measure the performance of your automated systems and make adjustments as needed. Analytics tools can help track key performance indicators (KPIs) such as website traffic, conversion rates, and customer engagement. I routinely review my analytics dashboards to see which marketing campaigns are performing best and which areas might need improvement. For you, staying on top of data is essential for refining your strategies and ensuring that your side hustles are as efficient as possible.

When you use technology to streamline your operations, you gain insights into what works and what does not. This continuous feedback loop allows you to optimize your processes, cut unnecessary costs, and reinvest in the areas that yield the highest returns. I learned early on that neglecting performance metrics could lead to missed opportunities for growth. For you, tracking performance data will help you fine-tune your revenue streams and achieve a higher level of efficiency over time.

Case Studies of Successful Passive Income Models

Learning from real examples can provide you with a blueprint for success. In this section, you will read about several case studies that illustrate how individuals have built successful passive income models through entrepreneurial ventures and side hustles. These stories offer practical insights and inspiration that you can apply to your own journey toward early retirement and tax-free income.

The Freelancer Turned Business Owner

One of the most common transitions is from a freelancer to a business owner. I met a professional who started as a freelance graphic designer, taking on small projects in the evenings. Over time, he built a reputation for quality work and began to receive referrals from satisfied clients. With a steady flow of projects, he decided to launch his own design agency. What began as a one-person operation gradually grew into a team of designers, and the income became more passive as he focused on managing the business rather than doing every design himself. His story is a powerful reminder that turning your freelance skills into a scalable business can create a significant, reliable income stream. For you, if you have a marketable skill, this approach can transform your income and provide the freedom to focus on higher-level strategies.

Digital Products and Online Courses

Another inspiring example comes from the world of digital products. An entrepreneur I know had a background in digital marketing and began by writing an eBook on proven marketing strategies. The eBook was a modest success, but he soon realized that his audience craved more in-depth training. He developed a series of online courses that broke down complex topics into digestible lessons. Once the courses were launched, they began generating regular sales with minimal ongoing effort on his part.

The courses were hosted on an online platform, and he automated most of the marketing and sales processes using email sequences and social media advertising. His passive income from digital products allowed him to reduce his working hours and focus on strategic planning for future projects. For you, creating digital products can be an excellent way to monetize your expertise and build an income stream that grows over time.

Real Estate Ventures Managed Online

Real estate is another field where technology has made a difference. One investor I worked with started by purchasing a few rental properties and managing them personally. As the portfolio grew, he began using property management software to handle tenant communications, maintenance scheduling, and rent collection.

Later, he invested in a small portfolio of properties in different regions, reducing his risk through diversification. The use of technology allowed him to manage multiple properties without the need for physical presence in each location. Eventually, he expanded his holdings by investing in real estate crowdfunding platforms and REITs, further diversifying his income. His journey shows that leveraging technology can transform traditional real estate investments into a more efficient and largely passive income source. For you, using online tools to manage and scale real estate ventures can be a powerful addition to your portfolio.

Affiliate Marketing and Content Creation

Another notable case involves affiliate marketing combined with content creation. A friend of mine started a blog focused on personal finance and early retirement strategies. She invested time in creating valuable content that resonated with a specific audience and built a steady readership. Over time, she integrated affiliate links into her posts and partnered with companies that offered products aligned with her blog's themes. The income from affiliate commissions grew steadily, and she eventually turned her blog into a full-time venture. By automating her content publishing and using analytics to fine-tune her marketing efforts, she managed to generate a significant stream of passive income. For you, if you enjoy writing or creating content, affiliate marketing is a way to turn your passion into a revenue source that supports your financial goals.

Combining Multiple Revenue Streams

One of the most powerful lessons from these case studies is the value of combining multiple revenue streams. Many successful entrepreneurs do not rely on a single source of income. Instead, they create a diverse portfolio of revenue streams—ranging from service-based income to digital products, affiliate marketing, and real estate—that work together to provide financial stability.

I have witnessed individuals who, by merging various strategies, achieve a level of income that is not dependent on any one channel. For you, the key is to experiment with different ideas and gradually build a mix that suits your skills, interests, and lifestyle. Over time, as each revenue stream matures, you can allocate more resources to scaling them further.

Lessons Learned and Best Practices

The stories shared in this section offer several lessons that you can apply to your own entrepreneurial ventures:

- **Start Small and Scale Gradually:** Many entrepreneurs begin with a small project and slowly reinvest profits to grow the business. This approach minimizes risk and allows you to learn from each step.

- **Focus on Automation:** The use of technology and automated systems is a recurring theme. Automating repetitive tasks not only saves time but also ensures consistency in income generation.

- **Diversify Your Income Sources:** Relying on one revenue stream can be risky. Multiple sources provide a buffer against fluctuations in any single market.

- **Reinvest in Your Ventures:** As your side hustles generate income, reinvesting profits to expand your operations is essential. This reinvestment accelerates growth and helps you build a larger income base.

- **Adapt to Market Trends:** Staying informed and flexible is key. Markets change, and the ability to adjust your strategies in response to new opportunities can set you apart.

- **Keep Learning:** Continuous education and self-improvement play significant roles in entrepreneurial success. Learn from your experiences and those of others, and use that knowledge to refine your approach.

For you, the path to entrepreneurial income and side hustles is paved with opportunities to harness your skills, use technology smartly, and create a system that supports your long-term goals. Each case study demonstrates that success does not come overnight—it is the result of persistent effort, careful planning, and the willingness to try new approaches. As you work on your projects, keep these lessons in mind, and let the experiences of others guide your decisions.

In this chapter, you have explored how entrepreneurial income and side hustles can transform your financial future by creating additional revenue streams, leveraging technology and automation, and learning from real-life examples of successful passive income models. You have seen that by using your skills and interests to generate extra income, you can reduce reliance on a single paycheck and accelerate your journey toward early retirement. Automation tools and digital platforms make it easier to manage these ventures, ensuring that your extra income grows with minimal ongoing effort.

Your entrepreneurial journey is not about rapid riches but about steady progress. Every new revenue stream you build, every process you automate, and every lesson you learn from successful models contributes to your overall financial stability. This chapter has shown you that smart strategies, persistence, and a willingness to experiment can lead to a diverse income portfolio that supports your long-term goals.

By actively pursuing side hustles and entrepreneurial ventures, you are taking control of your financial destiny. The extra income generated from these efforts can be reinvested into tax-free investment vehicles and savings strategies, further enhancing your ability to retire early and enjoy a secure, independent future. With each step, you build not only financial security but also the freedom to live life on your own terms.

As you move forward, remember that the key is to remain adaptable and open to new opportunities. Use technology to streamline your operations, monitor your progress, and refine your strategies based on performance data. Embrace both successes and setbacks as valuable learning experiences that will shape your approach over time.

Your journey toward entrepreneurial income is an ongoing process. Stay committed to exploring new ideas, scaling your revenue streams, and integrating them into a broader financial plan that minimizes taxes and maximizes returns. With dedication and smart planning, you have the power to create a resilient system that supports a tax-free retirement and a life of financial freedom.

Every side project you launch, every automated system you set up, and every case study you learn from brings you closer to a future where your money works for you. Your efforts today build the foundation for a secure tomorrow, where you enjoy the benefits of multiple income sources without sacrificing your lifestyle. Keep pushing forward, use your time wisely, and let your entrepreneurial spirit guide you toward the financial independence you deserve.

Chapter 8

Advanced Tax Optimization Techniques

This chapter tackles advanced strategies to reduce your tax burden while maximizing your wealth for early retirement and tax-free passive income. You will learn how to take advantage of legal deductions and loopholes, tailor strategies for high-income earners, and set up estate planning that secures your legacy for future generations. These techniques require careful attention and planning, but they are well within your reach when you break down each step. In this chapter, you will see how smart, informed decisions can turn tax rules into opportunities for wealth creation.

Legal Loopholes and Deductions to Use

Tax laws are filled with provisions that, if applied correctly, can greatly reduce your taxable income. You might feel that these rules are designed solely to complicate your financial life, but there are clear legal methods that allow you to reduce your tax liability without breaking any laws. When you learn to use these strategies effectively, you gain more control over your money, and more of your earnings work for you rather than going to taxes.

Uncovering Available Deductions

One of the simplest ways to lower your tax bill is by taking full advantage of deductions that you are legally entitled to claim. These deductions lower your taxable income and help you keep more of your earnings. For instance, expenses related to self-employment, such as home office costs, business travel, and certain education expenses, can be deducted if you meet the necessary criteria. I recall the relief I felt the first time I discovered that expenses I thought were personal actually qualified as business costs. This realization changed the way I managed my budget and boosted my savings significantly. Understanding what qualifies as a deductible expense is a powerful tool that reduces your tax burden and improves your overall cash flow.

The tax code offers deductions for contributions to retirement accounts, health savings accounts, and charitable donations. If you donate to a registered charity, you may be able to deduct the donated amount, reducing your taxable income. Keeping accurate records of these contributions is essential, as detailed documentation supports your claims when filing taxes. I once spent extra time organizing my receipts and bank statements, and it paid off during tax season when my deductions significantly lowered my tax liability. You, too, can benefit from maintaining clear records and filing your taxes in a way that captures every deduction available to you.

Using Legal Loopholes

While the term "loophole" may have negative connotations, it refers to legal strategies that take advantage of the tax code's specific provisions. These strategies can include shifting income to family members in lower tax brackets, using depreciation on investment properties, or employing strategies like cost segregation in real estate investments.

For example, if you own rental properties, cost segregation studies can reclassify certain building components into shorter depreciation periods, which accelerates the tax write-off and improves your cash flow.

I remember when I first implemented a cost segregation study on one of my properties, and the resulting tax savings allowed me to reinvest in further income-generating assets. Adopting such techniques can mean the difference between a high effective tax rate and one that is much lower, keeping more of your earnings intact.

Another effective strategy is shifting taxable income into tax-deferred or tax-exempt vehicles. This can be achieved by investing in accounts like a Roth IRA or other tax-advantaged accounts. Even if your income is high, you can use strategies that move taxable income into these accounts, delaying or eliminating taxes on investment growth. I once reallocated a portion of my portfolio into tax-deferred accounts and experienced a notable difference in my annual tax bill. For you, these strategies are essential if you want to build a retirement portfolio that minimizes tax drag and maximizes compounding returns over time.

Tracking Legislative Changes

Tax laws change regularly, and keeping up with new legislation is critical if you want to optimize your tax strategy continuously. You should set aside time each year to review tax law updates or consult with a tax professional who can guide you through the changes. I recall a year when new tax legislation altered the way certain deductions were calculated; a timely conversation with my advisor helped me adjust my strategy promptly, avoiding unexpected tax bills. For you, being proactive in understanding legislative updates ensures that your strategy remains current and effective.

Practical Steps to Optimize Deductions

- **Maintain Detailed Records:** Keep organized files of all receipts, invoices, and relevant documents. Detailed records support your deductions and protect you in the event of an audit.

- **Use Accounting Software:** Tools like QuickBooks or other financial management software can help you track expenses, categorize costs, and generate reports that highlight potential deductions.

- **Consult Professionals:** Engage a tax advisor who specializes in advanced strategies. Their expertise can reveal deductions and loopholes that you might overlook.

- **Review Your Investments:** Regularly analyze your investment portfolio to ensure that income-producing assets are structured in the most tax-efficient manner. Moving certain assets into tax-advantaged accounts can yield substantial savings over time.

- **Plan Charitable Contributions:** If you donate to charity, plan your contributions to maximize your deductions. Some donors benefit by bunching charitable contributions into one tax year to exceed standard deduction limits.

By following these steps, you can unlock deductions and legal strategies that reduce your taxable income. Every dollar saved on taxes is a dollar that can compound for your future, propelling you closer to a tax-free retirement.

Strategies for High-Income Earners

High-income earners face a unique set of challenges when it comes to tax optimization. You might find that as your income increases, so does your tax rate, making it more difficult to build wealth. However, there are advanced techniques that help you manage this situation effectively. By taking targeted actions, you can lower your effective tax rate and preserve more wealth for your future.

Income Shifting and Splitting

One method to manage high income is to shift income to family members in lower tax brackets. This technique, known as income splitting, involves legally transferring a portion of your income to a spouse or child who falls into a lower tax bracket. For example, if you own a business, you might employ your spouse or adult child, thereby allocating part of the income to them. I recall a time when I adjusted my business structure to include family members, and the resulting tax savings were significant. For you, income splitting is a practical way to reduce your overall tax liability, as long as you follow the legal guidelines to ensure that compensation is reasonable and documented.

Maximizing Retirement Contributions

For high-income earners, retirement accounts not only provide long-term security but also serve as powerful tax shelters. Contributing the maximum allowed to 401(k) plans, IRAs, and other tax-deferred vehicles reduces your current taxable income. I remember feeling a sense of accomplishment when I saw my 401(k) contributions lower my taxable income by a substantial amount, allowing more funds to be reinvested for growth. It is important to be aware of the contribution limits and take full advantage of any catch-up provisions if you are over the age of 50. The more you shelter your income, the more you can reduce the immediate tax burden, letting your money compound over time.

Employing Advanced Business Structures

High-income earners often benefit from structuring their businesses in ways that offer favorable tax treatment. This might involve forming an S-corporation or a limited liability company (LLC) to take advantage of deductions related to business expenses, health insurance premiums, and retirement contributions. I recall restructuring my business and learning how different entities could offer tax advantages that were not available to sole proprietors. Exploring these structures with the help of a knowledgeable advisor can open up new avenues for tax savings. By optimizing your business organization, you can reduce your overall tax burden while enjoying the benefits of increased operational efficiency.

Investment in Tax-Exempt Securities

Investing in tax-exempt securities, such as municipal bonds, is another strategy that high-income earners can use. Since these investments offer income that is free from federal (and sometimes state) taxes, they can help you generate returns without increasing your taxable income. I once reviewed my portfolio and realized that shifting a portion of my fixed-income investments into municipal bonds resulted in a noticeable reduction in my annual tax bill. This is an important strategy to balance your portfolio while also ensuring that a significant portion of your income remains untaxed. By carefully selecting tax-exempt investments, you can achieve a dual goal of income generation and tax efficiency.

Utilizing Health Savings Accounts (HSAs)

Health Savings Accounts offer triple tax benefits: contributions are tax-deductible, the account grows tax-free, and withdrawals for qualified medical expenses are tax-free. For high-income earners, HSAs are an underutilized resource that can provide both short-term and long-term benefits. I remember the relief of knowing that my HSA was not only covering healthcare expenses but also acting as an additional investment vehicle. For you, maximizing contributions to an HSA is a smart move, especially if you are in a high tax bracket. The funds in an HSA can be invested and grow over time, effectively reducing your taxable income while building a cushion for future medical expenses.

Strategic Charitable Giving

Charitable giving is another powerful tool for high-income earners. Beyond the personal satisfaction of supporting causes you care about, charitable contributions can provide substantial tax deductions. One advanced strategy is to establish a donor-advised fund (DAF). A DAF allows you to make a charitable contribution, take an immediate tax deduction, and then distribute the funds to charities over time. I once set up a donor-advised fund, and the process allowed me to optimize my charitable giving in a way that maximized tax benefits while supporting my favorite organizations. This strategy not only reduces your taxable income but also offers a structured approach to philanthropy that can be deeply rewarding.

Deferring Income and Accelerating Deductions

For high-income earners, the timing of income and deductions can be critical. If you have control over when you receive income or incur deductible expenses, you can manage your taxable income more efficiently. I once postponed receiving a bonus until the following year because I anticipated a lower tax rate then, and the decision resulted in significant savings. Deferring income into a lower-tax year and accelerating deductions into a higher-income year can smooth out the peaks and valleys of your tax liability. This strategy requires careful planning and coordination with your financial advisor, but it can be one of the most effective ways to reduce your overall tax burden.

Practical Steps for High-Income Tax Optimization

- **Review Your Business Structure:** Evaluate your current business entity and consult with a tax professional to determine if a restructuring could offer tax advantages.

- **Max Out Tax-Deferred Contributions:** Ensure you are contributing the maximum allowed to retirement accounts and HSAs.

- **Plan Income Timing:** If possible, adjust the timing of bonuses or other income to align with lower tax years.

- **Leverage Tax-Exempt Investments:** Add municipal bonds and other tax-exempt securities to your portfolio to generate untaxed income.

- **Document Expenses:** Keep thorough records of all deductible expenses and consult regularly with a tax advisor to update your strategy.

By following these steps, you can tailor your tax strategy to the unique challenges that come with high income. Every adjustment you make contributes to a lower effective tax rate and frees up more resources for building your retirement nest egg.

Estate Planning & Generational Wealth Transfer

The final piece of advanced tax optimization is planning for the future beyond your own retirement. Estate planning and generational wealth transfer ensure that the wealth you build is preserved for your heirs while minimizing the tax burden on your estate. This topic is often complex, but with careful planning, you can set up a strategy that benefits both you and your family.

Establishing a Comprehensive Estate Plan

A solid estate plan goes beyond writing a will. It involves organizing your assets, choosing the right beneficiaries, and setting up trusts that can protect your wealth from excessive taxation. I recall working with an estate planning attorney who explained how a properly structured trust could keep your assets out of probate and reduce estate taxes significantly. Having an estate plan in place provides peace of mind that your hard-earned wealth will be managed according to your wishes and transferred to your loved ones with minimal loss.

Trusts are one of the most powerful tools in estate planning. They allow you to control how and when your assets are distributed, often shielding them from estate taxes and creditors. A common strategy is the use of a revocable living trust, which gives you flexibility during your lifetime while ensuring that your estate is managed efficiently after you pass. I have seen many families benefit from establishing trusts that provide for both immediate needs and long-term goals. Setting up a trust can be an essential part of protecting your legacy and ensuring that your beneficiaries receive the maximum benefit from your estate.

Minimizing Estate Taxes

High net worth often comes with the challenge of estate taxes, which can take a large portion of your wealth before it reaches your heirs. There are several advanced techniques to minimize these taxes, such as gifting strategies, establishing irrevocable trusts, and making use of the lifetime gift tax exemption. I remember a time when I reviewed my estate plan and discovered that strategic gifts made during my lifetime could reduce the size of my taxable estate. These strategies are particularly important if your wealth exceeds the threshold for estate taxes. By transferring assets gradually over time or setting up trusts, you can lower the overall value of your taxable estate and leave more for your heirs.

Annual gift exclusions allow you to transfer a certain amount of money or property to each beneficiary without incurring gift taxes. This annual exclusion is a powerful tool when used consistently over the years. I once calculated how much I could gift each year to my children without affecting my lifetime exemption, and it provided a clear roadmap for reducing my taxable estate. Planning your gifts carefully is a key component of effective estate planning.

Planning for Generational Wealth Transfer

Beyond just minimizing taxes, estate planning is about ensuring that your wealth is managed wisely for future generations. This means not only transferring assets but also providing guidance on how those assets should be used. Some families set up family foundations or educational trusts to instill values of financial responsibility and support long-term goals.

I have met individuals who used their wealth to create scholarship funds and community initiatives, leaving a lasting legacy that extends beyond monetary value. Generational wealth transfer is an opportunity to make a lasting impact on your family and community. It requires open communication with your heirs and careful planning to avoid conflicts and ensure that your wishes are honored.

Involving Professionals in Your Estate Plan

Because estate planning involves a range of legal, tax, and financial issues, it is wise to work with professionals who specialize in this area. Estate planning attorneys, financial planners, and tax advisors can work together to craft a plan that meets your objectives. I recall sitting down with a team of experts who reviewed my entire financial picture, identifying areas where I could reduce tax liabilities and better protect my assets. Engaging professionals can save time, reduce mistakes, and ensure that your plan is robust enough to withstand changes in tax laws and family dynamics.

Best Practices for Estate Planning

- **Keep Your Documents Updated:** Life changes, and so do your financial circumstances. Review your will, trusts, and beneficiary designations regularly.

- **Plan for Liquidity:** Ensure that your estate includes liquid assets or insurance policies that can cover any estate taxes or debts, so your heirs do not have to sell off key assets.

- **Communicate with Your Family:** Transparency about your estate plan can help avoid disputes and ensure that your intentions are clear.

- **Utilize Trusts Strategically:** Trusts can protect assets from creditors and reduce estate taxes. They also provide control over how assets are distributed over time.

- **Maximize Gifting Opportunities:** Use annual gift exclusions and other strategies to gradually reduce your taxable estate while providing for your heirs.

By following these best practices, you not only protect your wealth from excessive taxation but also lay a strong foundation for your family's financial future. For you, estate planning is an ongoing process that requires regular attention and adjustments as circumstances change. When done correctly, it can ensure that your legacy endures and that the wealth you build continues to benefit future generations.

Advanced tax optimization is about taking full advantage of every legal strategy available to reduce your tax liability. In this chapter, you have learned techniques that range from unlocking deductions and legal strategies to managing the tax challenges of high income and planning for the future through estate planning. Each section has provided actionable steps and real-life examples to help you refine your approach.

You have seen how strategic use of deductions, income shifting, and smart investment structures can dramatically lower your tax rate. High-income earners can harness these strategies to preserve wealth, while advanced estate planning ensures that your assets are passed on to your loved ones with minimal losses. Each step you take in optimizing your taxes is an investment in your future—one that allows you to save more, invest more, and ultimately, retire with a tax-free income.

As you implement these advanced techniques, remember that staying informed and proactive is essential. Tax laws evolve, and what works today may need adjustments tomorrow. Make it a habit to review your strategy regularly, consult with professionals, and adjust your plan as needed. Your dedication to mastering these strategies will not only boost your current financial position but will also secure a stable, tax-efficient legacy for the future.

Your journey to a tax-free retirement is built on informed decisions and proactive management. Every legal deduction you claim, every strategy you adopt for high income, and every step you take in planning your estate brings you closer to the financial independence you desire. With each advanced technique, you gain more control over your wealth and set the stage for a future where taxes do not hold you back.

By using the strategies in this chapter, you are taking concrete steps to ensure that your money works as hard as you do. The path may require careful planning and regular adjustments, but the reward is a secure retirement and the peace of mind that comes with knowing you have optimized your finances to the fullest extent. Continue to educate yourself, work with trusted advisors, and refine your approach. Your efforts today will compound over time, ensuring that you not only achieve early retirement but also leave a lasting legacy for generations to come.

Embrace these advanced tax optimization techniques as part of your broader financial strategy. They are the tools that enable you to build a resilient, tax-free portfolio—one that grows steadily and supports your long-term goals. Every measure you implement to reduce your tax liability is a step toward a future where your income is maximized, your wealth is preserved, and your legacy is secured.

Your journey to financial freedom involves mastering these advanced strategies. With determination, careful planning, and the willingness to adapt as circumstances change, you can reduce your tax burden and build a solid foundation for your retirement. Keep your focus on the long-term benefits, and let each optimized tax strategy propel you toward the secure, tax-free retirement you deserve.

Free Goodwill

Congratulations! You've made it through this book, and I hope it has given you valuable insights into achieving financial freedom while legally minimizing taxes. Writing this book was an effort to share strategies that have helped countless people retire early and live off tax-free passive income. But now, I need **your help.**

Your Review Makes a Difference

If this book has provided you with useful strategies, practical tools, or even a fresh perspective on retirement planning, I would deeply appreciate it if you could take a moment to leave an honest review on **Amazon.**

Why? Because **your feedback helps others** decide if this book is right for them. When you share what you liked (or even what you think could be improved), you're helping future readers make informed choices. Reviews also encourage more people to take control of their financial future.

Leaving a review takes just a few minutes, but it makes a world of difference for both the author and potential readers. Whether it's a brief note about what you found helpful or a detailed review of your experience, I'd love to hear your thoughts.

To leave a review, simply:

1. Go to **Amazon** and find this book's page.

2. Scroll down to the **customer review section**.

3. Click **"Write a Review"**, rate the book, and share your thoughts.

Your support means the world, and I truly appreciate you taking the time to do this!

Continue Your Financial Journey

If you found this book helpful, I have another resource that might interest you:

Be Smart with Debt

Debt is often seen as the enemy of financial freedom, but **not all debt is bad.** In my book, **Be Smart with Debt,** I break down how to use debt wisely, eliminate harmful debt faster, and even leverage strategic debt for wealth-building.

Here's what you'll discover:

- The difference between **good debt** and **bad debt**
- How to pay off **high-interest debt** quickly without sacrificing your lifestyle
- Strategies for using **low-interest debt** to build wealth
- Ways to protect yourself from financial risks related to debt

Just like this book, **Be Smart with Debt** focuses on actionable strategies to help you take control of your finances and build lasting wealth.

If that sounds like something you'd find valuable, I'd love for you to check it out!

Thank You for Your Support

Writing a book is just the beginning—the real impact happens when readers like you take action. Thank you for allowing me to be part of your financial journey. Your support, your reviews, and your recommendations help this knowledge reach more people who need it.

Wishing you a future filled with financial security, freedom, and smart decision-making. Scan the QR Code to get your **Passive Income Quick-Start Guide** and **Tax-Free Retirement Blueprint.**

Chapter 9

Steering Through Market Cycles & Economic Shifts

This chapter is dedicated to helping you adjust your financial plan as markets change, manage risks for lasting success, and maintain a healthy balance between growth and asset preservation. When you face uncertain economic times or sudden shifts in market trends, you need strategies that keep your portfolio robust and flexible. You will learn techniques for modifying your approach during volatile periods, protecting your assets over the long term, and finding the right mix between aggressive growth and cautious preservation.

The insights shared here are based on practical experiences, personal lessons, and the wisdom gained from years of working with changing economic conditions. Every decision you make in response to market shifts brings you closer to a future where your income remains tax-free and your retirement goals stay within reach.

Adapting Your Plan in Volatile Markets

When the market shows signs of instability, your ability to adjust your investment plan can have a profound effect on your long-term financial success. There are moments when the value of your investments may drop unexpectedly, and these times test your resolve and planning. You have likely witnessed news headlines about market crashes or sudden shifts in economic policy. Such periods can be unsettling, but they also offer opportunities to reallocate your assets and improve your overall strategy.

Recognizing the Signs of Change

You may notice that market sentiment shifts as interest rates rise, economic data fluctuates, or geopolitical events cause uncertainty. In my early years as an investor, I recall a period when market values fell sharply due to unexpected global events. Although it was stressful at the time, I used that period to review my portfolio, reassess my asset allocation, and determine which investments still aligned with my long-term goals. The key is not to panic when market values drop. Instead, view these moments as chances to re-examine your strategy and take advantage of lower prices in quality investments.

As you review your portfolio during volatile periods, pay attention to which assets are under pressure and why. Some sectors may be hit harder than others, and sometimes these declines are temporary. You might find that companies with strong fundamentals experience a short-term setback. Reflect on your investments' performance over several market cycles rather than reacting to a single drop in value. Over time, I learned that staying focused on the long-term picture allowed me to buy additional shares of quality stocks at attractive prices, ultimately boosting my returns when the market recovered.

Adjusting Asset Allocation

One method to adapt in volatile markets is by shifting your asset allocation. You can reassign funds from investments that are more sensitive to market swings into those that offer more stability or tax advantages. For example, if you notice that equities in certain industries have become overvalued, you may move some capital into fixed-income instruments or tax-advantaged accounts. I once rebalanced my portfolio during a period of high volatility, reducing my exposure to aggressive growth stocks and increasing my holdings in dividend-paying companies and municipal bonds. This adjustment helped cushion my portfolio against further declines while preserving the potential for long-term gains.

When you decide to adjust your asset allocation, use a systematic approach. Create a target allocation that reflects your risk tolerance and long-term objectives, and then stick to that plan as much as possible. Although market fluctuations might tempt you to change tactics frequently, discipline is essential. I learned from experience that frequent, emotion-driven adjustments often lead to higher transaction costs and lower overall returns. Instead, focus on a well-defined plan, rebalancing periodically—perhaps once or twice a year—to ensure that your portfolio remains aligned with your goals even in turbulent times.

Tactical Opportunities During Downturns

Volatile markets are not just a challenge—they can also be a chance to improve your portfolio. You may find opportunities to acquire high-quality assets at discounted prices. I recall a specific period when market sentiment was very negative, and many investors were selling off assets at low prices. I used that time to purchase shares of companies with a long history of steady performance. By locking in a lower price, I not only increased my holdings but also set the stage for greater long-term growth. For you, adopting a contrarian mindset during market downturns can yield impressive results if you remain calm and focused.

When exploring these opportunities, thorough research is essential. Look for companies with solid balance sheets, strong management teams, and products or services that remain in demand despite market conditions. Even in a volatile market, some investments are undervalued simply because of widespread fear.

The challenge is to separate short-term market sentiment from the underlying value of an asset. Rely on data, fundamental analysis, and your own experience rather than rumors or panic. Once you have identified potential opportunities, you might decide to increase your exposure gradually rather than making a large, sudden purchase. This approach helps you manage risk while still taking advantage of lower prices.

Reassessing Your Long-Term Goals

During times of economic uncertainty, it is important to step back and revisit your long-term goals. Ask yourself whether your overall strategy still aligns with your vision for early retirement and tax-free income. I remember a period of severe market turbulence when I took time off from the daily market fluctuations to re-read my financial goals and re-assess my risk tolerance. That exercise helped me reaffirm my commitment to a long-term plan and adjust minor details rather than overhauling my entire strategy. Keeping your long-term goals in focus can prevent you from making impulsive decisions during temporary market setbacks.

If you find that your goals have shifted because of changes in your personal life or economic conditions, update your plan accordingly. Adjust your risk profile, review your time horizon, and, if necessary, modify your asset allocation. Taking time to realign your goals with your current situation helps you maintain discipline and avoid the temptation to react hastily to short-term market movements. Each time you revisit your long-term objectives, you build a more resilient plan that can withstand the ups and downs of the market.

Staying Informed and Seeking Guidance

Finally, adapting your plan in volatile markets requires that you remain well-informed about economic trends and market developments. You might subscribe to reputable financial newsletters, attend seminars, or follow trusted experts who offer insights into market cycles. I have found that regular engagement with financial literature and professional advice has been invaluable in shaping my approach during periods of market uncertainty. For you, continuous learning and consultation with knowledgeable advisors can help you identify early warning signs and adjust your strategy before small issues become significant problems.

Regular discussions with a financial advisor can provide clarity during volatile times. These professionals help you interpret market signals and recommend adjustments tailored to your individual situation. Even if you are confident in your own analysis, an external perspective can reinforce your decisions and offer alternative strategies you might not have thought of. Trusting expert advice when you face complex market conditions can be a key factor in preserving your wealth and staying on track for early retirement.

Risk Management Strategies for Long-Term Success

Managing risk is essential when you aim for long-term financial security. Every investment comes with some degree of risk, and your ability to mitigate those risks will determine whether you reach your retirement goals. In this section, you will learn how to identify, measure, and manage risk so that your portfolio remains strong over time.

Diversification as a Shield

One of the simplest ways to manage risk is by spreading your investments across various asset classes. You may allocate your portfolio among stocks, bonds, real estate, and alternative investments to reduce exposure to any single source of risk. I remember when I first understood the importance of diversification; my portfolio used to be heavily weighted in one sector, and a downturn in that industry led to significant losses. By broadening my investments across different areas, I was able to smooth out the impact of market declines and protect my overall returns. Building a diversified portfolio is one of the most effective methods to shield yourself from sudden shocks.

When you diversify, aim for a balance that aligns with your risk tolerance. Some assets may provide high growth potential but come with increased volatility, while others offer steady income with lower risk. Creating a mix that suits your financial goals is a dynamic process that may require adjustments over time. It is helpful to review your portfolio periodically and ensure that no single asset class dominates. I learned to rebalance my investments regularly, which kept my risk levels in check while allowing me to capture growth opportunities in different market segments. Regular rebalancing is an essential discipline that helps you maintain control over your overall risk exposure.

Hedging and Protective Strategies

Beyond diversification, there are specific hedging strategies that you can employ to protect your portfolio from market downturns. For example, options contracts can serve as insurance against significant declines in stock prices. I once used protective put options during a period of anticipated volatility, which provided a safety net that limited my losses when the market dropped sharply. While options trading requires a learning curve and may not be suitable for everyone, it is a useful tool if you are comfortable with more advanced techniques.

Another hedging strategy involves investing in assets that typically perform well during economic downturns, such as gold or certain defensive stocks. These investments tend to hold their value when other parts of the market are suffering, acting as a counterbalance to more volatile assets. I experimented with a small allocation to precious metals during uncertain times, and that portion of my portfolio helped mitigate the overall impact of market declines. Using a mix of hedging instruments can enhance your risk management strategy and provide additional stability during turbulent periods.

Setting Stop-Loss Orders and Limit Orders

Risk management also involves setting clear exit strategies for your investments. Stop-loss orders are an effective way to protect against significant losses by automatically selling a security when it falls below a predetermined price. I have used stop-loss orders to shield my portfolio from unexpected drops, and they have proven invaluable in preserving capital during rapid market declines. For you, establishing these thresholds is an important part of risk management. By setting stop-loss orders, you remove the emotional aspect of decision-making during volatile times and create a safety mechanism that limits potential losses.

Limit orders can also help you manage risk by ensuring that you buy or sell assets only at prices that meet your criteria. When you use limit orders, you set a specific price at which you are willing to trade, preventing you from accepting unfavorable prices during periods of high volatility. I remember a time when I placed limit orders on several stocks during a market dip, and this approach allowed me to enter positions at attractive prices without worrying about rapid price fluctuations. Using these orders is a practical way to maintain control over your transactions and prevent impulsive decisions that might hurt your long-term strategy.

Stress Testing and Scenario Analysis

Another important aspect of risk management is to perform stress tests and scenario analyses on your portfolio. These exercises help you understand how your investments might react under various economic conditions, such as a recession, a spike in interest rates, or a sudden market crash. I recall running several hypothetical scenarios on my portfolio to see how different asset classes would perform during a crisis. The insights gained from these exercises enabled me to make adjustments before any real damage occurred. Stress-testing your portfolio provides valuable information about potential weaknesses and areas where additional protection might be needed.

Use tools and models that simulate different market conditions to assess the resilience of your portfolio. By testing various scenarios, you can identify which assets are most vulnerable and take corrective actions. This proactive approach helps you build a portfolio that can withstand severe market shifts while still offering growth potential. When you review the results of your stress tests, take time to adjust your asset allocation, hedging strategies, or even your exposure to certain sectors. The goal is to ensure that your portfolio remains balanced and capable of handling adverse events.

The Role of Liquidity in Risk Management

Maintaining a portion of your portfolio in liquid assets is a fundamental risk management strategy. Liquidity gives you the flexibility to respond to unexpected opportunities or to cover expenses without having to sell investments at unfavorable prices. I learned firsthand the value of liquidity during a period when market conditions were uncertain, and having readily available cash allowed me to take advantage of attractive buying opportunities. Keeping a cash reserve or highly liquid investments can serve as an emergency fund and reduce the pressure to liquidate long-term assets during market downturns.

A healthy liquidity position ensures that you can meet short-term obligations and avoid forced sales when market conditions are poor. Monitor your cash levels regularly and adjust them based on your risk tolerance and upcoming needs. In volatile markets, liquidity becomes even more valuable, as it provides the freedom to move quickly without incurring excessive transaction costs or tax liabilities.

Building a Long-Term Risk Management Plan

Risk management is not a one-time task; it is a continuous process that requires attention and regular adjustment. Over the years, I have developed a risk management plan that includes regular portfolio reviews, setting clear investment limits, and using automated systems to alert me to significant changes.

For you, establishing a formal risk management plan can provide structure and discipline. Write down your risk tolerance, set target allocations for different asset classes, and establish procedures for rebalancing and hedging. By documenting your plan, you create a reference that guides your decisions during both calm and turbulent periods.

As you build your long-term risk management plan, remember that the goal is not to eliminate risk entirely but to control it in a way that supports your financial goals. Effective risk management enables you to pursue growth opportunities while safeguarding your investments from severe losses. Each step you take to protect your portfolio contributes to a more resilient strategy that can endure economic shifts and market cycles.

Balancing Growth and Preservation in Your Portfolio

Achieving a balance between growth and preservation is one of the most important challenges you will face as you build your retirement portfolio. Growth-oriented investments can provide high returns but often come with higher volatility, while preservation-focused investments offer stability but may not generate substantial returns. Finding the right mix between these two objectives is key to meeting your long-term financial goals.

Defining Your Growth Objectives

When you set out to build wealth, you have goals that require your investments to grow at a reasonable pace. You might aim to double your money over several decades or generate sufficient income through capital appreciation and dividends. In my early years, I focused heavily on growth stocks and high-yield investments, eager to maximize returns. However, as my portfolio grew and my priorities shifted toward a secure retirement, I learned that unchecked pursuit of growth could expose me to unnecessary risk. It is important to define clear growth objectives that align with your time horizon and risk appetite.

Evaluate your current investments and assess how well they contribute to your growth goals. Look at historical performance, volatility, and the potential for future expansion. High-growth sectors, such as technology or emerging markets, might offer exciting prospects but can also experience significant swings. Balancing these with more stable investments can create a foundation that supports long-term growth without undue risk. I found that mixing growth stocks with stable dividend payers helped me maintain a steady upward trend in my portfolio while keeping risk at a manageable level.

Preservation: Protecting Your Capital

Preserving your capital is equally important as seeking growth. You want to ensure that the wealth you accumulate is not eroded by market downturns or unexpected expenses. Fixed-income securities, high-quality bonds, and cash equivalents serve as anchors in your portfolio during turbulent times. I learned this lesson when a portion of my portfolio, dedicated solely to aggressive investments, suffered heavy losses during a market correction. Shifting part of my assets into preservation-oriented investments not only reduced my overall risk but also provided a cushion during downturns. Including a significant preservation component in your portfolio is crucial to protect the gains you have worked hard to achieve.

Preservation strategies often involve accepting lower returns in exchange for lower risk. These investments may not offer the explosive growth potential of stocks, but they provide steady income and stability. Maintaining a percentage of your portfolio in conservative assets ensures that you have funds available when the market turns negative. This balance is essential for long-term success, as it allows you to ride out economic cycles without compromising your overall financial plan.

Finding the Right Allocation

Balancing growth and preservation is an ongoing process that requires regular adjustment. Your ideal allocation may change as you age, as market conditions evolve, or as your financial goals shift. I have adjusted my asset mix several times over the years—once I was more aggressive in my twenties, then gradually shifting toward a more balanced approach as I approached retirement age. For you, setting a target allocation based on your current circumstances and revisiting it periodically is a wise strategy. Use clear metrics to decide when to rebalance, such as fixed percentage thresholds or specific changes in market conditions.

One effective approach is to use a glide path—a strategy that gradually shifts your portfolio from growth-oriented assets to more conservative ones as you get closer to your target retirement date. This method helps you lock in gains and reduce risk as your financial needs become more immediate. I implemented a glide path in my own portfolio and found that it provided a structured way to adjust risk over time without making drastic changes in a short period. For you, a glide path can serve as a roadmap for balancing growth and preservation in a systematic and disciplined manner.

Incorporating Alternative Assets

While stocks and bonds form the backbone of most portfolios, alternative investments can play a vital role in balancing growth and preservation. Real estate, commodities, and even certain types of private equity can offer diversification that smooths out the ups and downs of the broader market. I once added a small allocation of alternative assets to my portfolio, and the effect was a reduction in overall volatility. For you, exploring alternative investments can be a way to achieve returns that are less correlated with traditional asset classes, further enhancing the stability of your portfolio.

When you incorporate alternatives, be mindful of their unique risk profiles and liquidity characteristics. Some alternatives, like real estate, require more active management and may not be as liquid as stocks or bonds. Ensure that your overall portfolio remains balanced and that you have sufficient liquid assets to meet short-term needs. Diversifying across asset classes not only contributes to growth but also provides a buffer during economic downturns, ensuring that your portfolio remains resilient.

Monitoring and Adjusting for Inflation

A key factor in balancing growth and preservation is protecting your portfolio against inflation. Inflation erodes the purchasing power of your money over time, so your investments need to outpace rising prices. I once realized that even though my portfolio was growing in nominal terms, my real returns were being eroded by inflation. This led me to reallocate some assets into investments that typically perform well in an inflationary environment, such as real estate and certain stocks with pricing power. Monitoring inflation and adjusting your asset allocation accordingly is essential to ensure that your wealth maintains its value over time.

Tools and Techniques for Ongoing Balance

There are several tools you can use to help maintain the balance between growth and preservation. Portfolio tracking software, risk assessment models, and regular consultations with financial advisors all play a role in keeping your strategy on track. I have relied on these resources to provide clarity during periods of market uncertainty, and they have been invaluable in making objective decisions. Using such tools can reduce the emotional stress of managing a portfolio and provide data-driven insights to guide your adjustments. Automated rebalancing services are available from many investment platforms, and these can help ensure that your portfolio remains aligned with your long-term goals without constant manual intervention.

As you steer through the ever-changing economic landscape, your ability to adjust your plan in volatile markets, manage risk, and strike a healthy balance between growth and preservation is critical to achieving long-term financial security and a tax-free retirement. This chapter has outlined practical methods for adapting your plan when markets shift unexpectedly, employing robust risk management strategies, and blending growth with asset protection in your portfolio. Each of these elements is a vital part of a disciplined strategy that enables you to maintain control over your finances even during uncertain times.

Your experiences with market cycles and economic shifts are opportunities to learn and refine your approach. Reflect on the lessons you have learned from past downturns and use them to build a more resilient plan. When you take proactive steps to adjust your asset allocation, use hedging techniques, set clear stop-loss measures, and integrate alternative investments, you not only safeguard your wealth but also position yourself to capitalize on future opportunities.

By continuously monitoring your investments, rebalancing your portfolio, and staying informed about economic trends, you build a strategy that remains robust over time. Remember that the balance between growth and preservation is dynamic and must be adjusted as your circumstances change. Whether you are using a glide path, incorporating alternatives, or relying on liquidity to seize opportunities, each decision you make today strengthens your financial future.

Your journey toward early retirement and tax-free passive income depends on your willingness to learn, adjust, and remain disciplined in the face of market volatility. The strategies presented in this chapter are designed to help you manage risk, protect your assets, and achieve sustainable growth. Every adjustment you implement in response to market changes is a step toward greater financial independence.

As you put these advanced risk management and portfolio balancing techniques into practice, keep your long-term goals at the forefront. With regular reviews, careful planning, and a commitment to staying informed, you can maintain a resilient portfolio that grows steadily over time while minimizing losses during downturns. Your financial future is built on the foundation of smart decisions made today—decisions that allow you to preserve your wealth, capture growth opportunities, and ensure that your retirement remains both secure and tax-free.

Embrace the challenge of managing market cycles and economic shifts as a part of your overall financial strategy. Each period of uncertainty is an opportunity to refine your approach, enhance your risk controls, and adjust your investments to better meet your long-term objectives. With persistence, discipline, and a willingness to learn from every experience, you can create a robust financial plan that withstands even the most turbulent economic times.

Every action you take to balance risk and growth, protect your capital, and adapt to market changes is a direct investment in your future. Trust in the process, lean on professional guidance when needed, and remain flexible as you progress on your path to a tax-free retirement. Your efforts today will yield the financial freedom you deserve tomorrow.

Conclusion

In this final chapter, you are given a clear wrap-up of the ideas and strategies that can help you reach a tax-free retirement and a life of financial freedom. This conclusion will summarize the key strategies for achieving a tax-free retirement, offer practical steps to get started immediately, and provide guidance on keeping your plan effective throughout your lifetime. The insights in this chapter are drawn from real-life experiences and careful planning. They are designed to help you build a future where you have full control over your income, investments, and ultimately, your retirement.

Recap: Key Strategies for a Tax-Free Retirement

Your journey toward a tax-free retirement involves multiple layers of smart financial choices. You have learned that a tax-free retirement is attainable when you adopt a combination of methods that work together to preserve your income and maximize returns. Let's review the main strategies that can transform your financial landscape.

Smart Use of Tax-Advantaged Accounts

You have discovered that retirement vehicles like Roth IRAs, Traditional IRAs, 401(k)s, and other tax-advantaged plans play a crucial role in building a tax-free income stream. By directing your savings into these accounts, you effectively reduce your taxable income and protect your investment growth from the erosive effect of taxes. For instance, putting money into a Roth IRA means that your investments grow tax-free and withdrawals are not taxed when you retire. This method has been a turning point for many investors, including myself, who realized that even modest contributions can compound into significant wealth over time. Your ability to allocate funds into these accounts is one of the pillars of your overall strategy.

Building Passive Income Streams

Another critical element in your journey is generating passive income. You have explored various avenues—from dividend stocks, ETFs, and index funds to real estate investments like rental properties and REITs, and even alternative income sources like peer-to-peer lending and digital products. These income streams provide a constant flow of cash without requiring you to trade time for money continuously. I recall the moment when my first dividend check arrived; it was a tangible reminder that my money was working for me. By reinvesting these earnings and letting them grow, you set up a cycle that propels you toward early retirement.

Tax Optimization and Investment Structuring

You also learned advanced strategies for optimizing your taxes. Tactics such as making full use of legal deductions, shifting income to lower-tax brackets, and using tax-efficient investment vehicles can dramatically reduce the tax drag on your portfolio. Techniques like tax-loss harvesting and smart asset location have empowered you to preserve your capital and maximize the growth potential of your investments. I remember the relief that came when I first restructured my portfolio; the visible drop in my tax bill was proof that proactive planning works. For you, these advanced strategies mean that every dollar saved on taxes is a dollar that can fuel your journey toward financial independence.

Entrepreneurial Income and Side Hustles

The drive to create additional revenue streams is another cornerstone of your plan. You have seen how pursuing side hustles or entrepreneurial ventures not only supplements your primary income but also speeds up your ability to invest in tax-free vehicles. Whether you use your skills to provide freelance services or develop a digital product that generates royalties, these efforts compound over time. I remember when I started working on projects outside my day job; each extra dollar earned made a meaningful difference in my investment portfolio. Your initiative in developing side businesses strengthens your overall financial strategy by providing extra capital that can be reinvested in growth and tax-free investments.

Risk Management and Portfolio Balance

You have understood the importance of managing risk in your portfolio. Through diversification, hedging, and careful asset allocation, you have built a system that protects your investments against market downturns and economic shifts. The key is to maintain the right balance between growth-oriented assets and those that preserve your capital. Reflecting on my own experiences during volatile markets, I learned that disciplined rebalancing and a focus on long-term goals can make all the difference. For you, a robust risk management plan is essential to keep your portfolio stable during uncertain times while still allowing for meaningful growth.

Estate Planning and Legacy Building

Finally, ensuring that your wealth is transferred efficiently to your loved ones is part of the tax-free retirement plan. Effective estate planning, including the use of trusts and gifting strategies, minimizes estate taxes and secures a legacy for future generations. I have seen how well-crafted estate plans have helped families keep more of their wealth intact. For you, taking steps to plan your estate early in your journey not only protects your assets but also provides peace of mind knowing that your hard work will benefit those you care about.

Action Steps to Start Today

Every journey begins with action. The strategies you have absorbed in this book are powerful, but their impact depends on the steps you take starting today. Use these actionable steps as your guide to put the plan into motion and build a path toward financial freedom.

1. Review Your Current Financial Picture

Begin by taking a detailed look at your finances. Gather all your income statements, investment accounts, and expense records. Create a summary that shows your current savings rate, investment allocations, and tax liabilities. I recall the clarity I achieved when I first organized my financial data; it was a wake-up call that helped me see where I could improve. For you, understanding your starting point is essential to measure progress and make informed adjustments.

2. Set Specific, Measurable Goals

Establish clear objectives for your retirement and income goals. Write down how much you want to save, the desired timeline for retirement, and the sources of passive income you plan to develop. You might decide to allocate a certain percentage of your monthly income to retirement accounts or set a target for building a diversified portfolio. I found that writing my goals down and reviewing them regularly kept me motivated and focused on the long-term vision. For you, clear goals serve as both a roadmap and a reminder of the progress you need to achieve.

3. Maximize Contributions to Tax-Advantaged Accounts

If you haven't already, increase your contributions to tax-advantaged accounts such as Roth IRAs, Traditional IRAs, and 401(k)s. Adjust your budget to ensure that you are saving as much as possible within these vehicles. I remember the satisfaction of seeing my tax savings grow as I pushed myself to contribute more each month. For you, this is a fundamental step that not only reduces your taxable income today but also sets the stage for tax-free withdrawals in the future.

4. Create or Enhance Your Passive Income Streams

Take inventory of your skills and resources that can be used to generate passive income. If you have an idea for a side hustle or an entrepreneurial project, outline a simple business plan. Begin small and scale up gradually. Use technology and automation tools to reduce manual work and ensure consistency. I started with one small project in my spare time and gradually built multiple streams of income that now support my lifestyle. For you, even a modest start can lead to substantial results over time as you reinvest and expand your ventures.

5. Optimize Your Investment Strategy

Review your portfolio to ensure that you are making the most tax-efficient choices. Evaluate whether your assets are allocated in the most effective manner, and consider techniques such as tax-loss harvesting, income shifting, and strategic asset location. I recall the moment when I shifted some investments into tax-free accounts and experienced a significant improvement in my net returns. For you, optimizing your investment strategy is about making sure every decision contributes to your long-term financial independence.

6. Develop a Risk Management Plan

Set up a risk management plan that includes regular portfolio reviews, stop-loss orders, and diversification targets. Use tools and software to monitor your investments and get alerts when it's time to rebalance. I have learned that consistent risk management can save you from panic during market downturns. For you, having a clear plan to manage risk not only protects your assets but also provides peace of mind when markets are unpredictable.

7. Engage with Professionals

If you feel overwhelmed or uncertain, seek guidance from financial advisors, tax professionals, and estate planners. Even a single consultation can offer insights that save you thousands in taxes and mistakes later. I have benefited greatly from the expertise of professionals who helped refine my strategies and align them with my goals. For you, expert advice is an investment in your future, ensuring that you make informed decisions at every step.

8. Set Up Regular Reviews

Schedule a regular review of your financial plan—quarterly or annually—to assess your progress, make adjustments, and update your goals as necessary. I set aside time each year to sit down with my financial records and rework my strategy; this habit has been critical to my ongoing success. For you, a periodic review keeps your plan relevant and ensures that you remain on track for a tax-free retirement.

9. Educate Yourself Continuously

The world of finance is ever-changing, and staying informed is key. Subscribe to trusted financial news sources, attend seminars, or join local investor groups to keep up with new strategies and regulatory changes. I have found that continuous education not only broadens my perspective but also introduces me to innovative techniques that enhance my plan. For you, ongoing learning is a valuable asset that empowers you to adapt to changes and seize new opportunities.

10. Commit to a Long-Term Mindset

Finally, make a commitment to yourself and your future. Understand that building a tax-free retirement is a marathon, not a sprint. There will be ups and downs, but your persistence and disciplined actions will pay off over time. I have experienced both setbacks and breakthroughs on my journey, and every challenge taught me something valuable about resilience and focus. For you, a long-term mindset ensures that every step you take today contributes to the secure, independent future you desire.

Maintaining Your Plan for a Lifetime of Freedom

Achieving a tax-free retirement is not the end of your financial journey—it is the foundation for a lifetime of freedom. Once you have set up your strategies, it is essential to maintain and adjust your plan as circumstances evolve. Here are some guidelines to help you sustain your financial independence over the long run.

Consistent Monitoring and Adaptation

The economic landscape will change over time. New tax laws, shifts in market dynamics, and changes in your personal life may require you to tweak your plan. It is important that you review your financial strategy at least once a year and adjust your allocations and contributions accordingly. I have made it a habit to spend a day every year reviewing my portfolio, assessing my goals, and making small but impactful changes. For you, regular monitoring is the key to ensuring that your strategy remains effective and relevant.

Setting Up Systems for Automatic Adjustments

One of the smartest ways to maintain your plan is to use technology to your advantage. Automatic contributions to retirement accounts, scheduled portfolio rebalancing, and alerts for significant market changes help you stay on track without constant manual intervention. I recall the relief I felt when I set up automatic transfers from my checking account to my investment accounts—this small system removed the daily stress of managing my savings. For you, automated systems not only save time but also enforce discipline, ensuring that your plan is executed consistently regardless of market conditions.

Continual Risk Management

Risk management is not a one-time task. As your assets grow and your circumstances change, the risk profile of your portfolio will shift. You must remain vigilant by periodically reassessing your risk tolerance, especially as you get closer to retirement. I have adjusted my asset allocation over the years to reflect a more conservative stance as my financial goals shifted. For you, staying in tune with your risk appetite and making adjustments as needed will help protect your hard-earned wealth and preserve the income you need for a comfortable retirement.

Reinvesting and Reinforcing Your Income Streams

Passive income streams are the backbone of a tax-free retirement plan. It is essential that you continually reinvest your earnings to boost your wealth over time. Whether it is reinvesting dividends, expanding your side business, or allocating additional funds to rental properties, the act of reinvestment amplifies your progress. I remember reinvesting every dividend check I received and watching my portfolio grow steadily as a result. For you, reinvestment is a powerful tool to accelerate your journey toward financial freedom while maintaining a tax-efficient structure.

Preparing for Life Changes

Your personal circumstances—such as changes in your career, family status, or health—can impact your financial strategy. It is important to have contingency plans in place so that you can adjust your plan without losing momentum. I once faced unexpected changes in my work schedule and had to adjust my savings rate temporarily; having a flexible plan allowed me to make those changes without derailing my overall goals. For you, building flexibility into your plan means that you are always prepared for life's unpredictable turns while staying focused on your long-term objectives.

Seeking Ongoing Professional Guidance

Even as you grow more confident in managing your finances, periodic consultations with financial advisors, tax professionals, and estate planners can provide valuable insights and keep your plan updated. I continue to meet with my advisors annually, not because I lack knowledge, but because the professional perspective often uncovers opportunities for further improvement. For you, regular professional reviews ensure that your strategy remains aligned with current best practices and any changes in laws or market conditions.

Cultivating a Growth Mindset

Maintaining your plan over a lifetime is as much about mindset as it is about strategy. Stay open to new ideas, be willing to make adjustments, and learn from both successes and setbacks. I have learned that every challenge I faced was an opportunity to refine my approach, and that persistence pays off in the long run. For you, a growth mindset ensures that you remain resilient, continuously improve your financial strategies, and never lose sight of your goal: a secure, tax-free retirement that supports a lifetime of freedom.

Building a Support Network

Surround yourself with people who share your financial vision. Joining investment clubs, online communities, or even informal groups of like-minded individuals can provide inspiration and accountability. I have found that discussing strategies with others helps me stay motivated and often leads to discovering new approaches that I hadn't thought of on my own. For you, building a support network is a way to maintain momentum and stay informed about new opportunities that can enhance your plan.

Keeping Detailed Records and Setting Milestones

Document your progress meticulously. Keep track of your savings rates, investment performance, and changes in your tax situation. Setting milestones along the way can help you gauge your progress and celebrate the achievements that mark each step forward. I remember the sense of accomplishment I felt each time I hit a savings milestone—it reinforced my commitment and motivated me to continue pushing forward. For you, setting measurable goals and tracking your progress provides a roadmap for long-term success.

Balancing Enjoyment and Discipline

Your plan is designed not just to secure your retirement, but also to give you the freedom to enjoy life without financial worries. It is important that you strike a balance between disciplined saving and investing and the freedom to enjoy the present. I have learned that a well-balanced life includes both hard work and moments of reward. For you, maintaining that balance ensures that your financial strategy supports a lifestyle that is both secure and fulfilling.

Final Thoughts

You now have a comprehensive view of how to achieve a tax-free retirement through smart saving, diversified investments, proactive tax planning, entrepreneurial ventures, and risk management. Every strategy and action step in this book builds toward the ultimate goal: a future where you are free from the burdens of excessive taxes and financial worry. The journey may be challenging, but each step you take reinforces your commitment to a future where you have full control over your financial destiny.

Reflect on the lessons you have learned. Recall the moments when careful planning and decisive action led to tangible results. Remember that every strategy is a tool in your toolkit—whether it is maximizing your tax-advantaged accounts, generating passive income, or planning your estate. Each tool, when used wisely, contributes to a secure, independent retirement. Your determination and discipline will compound over time, turning your aspirations into reality.

Today, you have the opportunity to put these strategies into action. By reviewing your finances, setting clear goals, maximizing contributions, diversifying your income, and managing risk with precision, you create a robust framework for long-term success. Use the action steps outlined above as a guide to start immediately. Even if the changes seem small at first, every decision you make builds a foundation for the future you want to achieve.

Your journey toward a tax-free retirement is a long-term project—one that requires continuous attention, regular reviews, and the flexibility to adjust as life changes. Keep your focus on the big picture, but do not neglect the small, everyday actions that contribute to your overall success. Trust in your plan, seek advice when needed, and always be open to learning. Your dedication today will ensure that you not only reach your retirement goals but also maintain a lifetime of financial freedom.

As you move forward, remember that your financial future is not set in stone. It evolves with every choice you make. Remain proactive, stay informed about changes in tax laws and market conditions, and be ready to adjust your strategy. The freedom you seek comes from a commitment to smart, disciplined actions—actions that allow you to work less for more and enjoy life on your own terms.

You have the tools, strategies, and mindset needed to achieve your goals. Now it is up to you to implement them, adapt as needed, and remain steadfast in your pursuit of financial independence. With each step you take, you reinforce the security of your future and pave the way for a retirement that is both fulfilling and tax-free.

Your journey may be challenging at times, but every moment spent working toward your goals is an investment in your freedom. Stay focused, be disciplined, and know that the strategies you have learned here are designed to empower you for a lifetime of financial well-being.

Your path to a tax-free retirement is built on a foundation of careful planning, proactive management, and a willingness to adapt. Use the key strategies, take decisive action today, and maintain your plan with regular reviews and adjustments. Your financial freedom is within reach, and every step you take brings you closer to a future where you control your income, protect your wealth, and enjoy a lifetime of security.

Embrace the journey with confidence. Each action you take is a step toward living a life where your money works for you—providing the freedom to pursue your passions, support your family, and enjoy every moment without financial stress. Your future is bright, and with the strategies and action steps outlined here, you are well-prepared to make that future a reality.

Appendices

Glossary of Terms

This glossary provides definitions for key financial and tax-related terms used throughout the book.

A

Adjusted Gross Income (AGI) – Your total income minus specific deductions, used to determine your taxable income.

Asset Allocation – The strategy of dividing investments among different asset classes (stocks, bonds, real estate) to balance risk and reward.

Annuity – A financial product that provides a steady income stream, often used for retirement planning.

B

Bond – A fixed-income investment where an investor lends money to a government or corporation in exchange for periodic interest payments.

Budgeting – The process of creating a plan to manage income and expenses efficiently.

Brokerage Account – An investment account that allows you to buy and sell stocks, bonds, ETFs, and mutual funds.

C

Capital Gains – The profit made from selling an asset (stocks, real estate) for more than its purchase price.

Compound Interest – Interest calculated on both the initial principal and the accumulated interest from previous periods.

Custodial Account – A financial account managed by a parent or guardian on behalf of a minor.

D

Dividend – A portion of a company's earnings distributed to shareholders, usually in cash or additional shares.

Diversification – A strategy of spreading investments across multiple assets to reduce risk.

Deferred Taxes – Taxes that are postponed to a future date, typically in retirement accounts like a Traditional IRA or 401(k).

E

Emergency Fund – Savings set aside to cover unexpected expenses, such as job loss or medical emergencies.

ETF (Exchange-Traded Fund) – A type of investment fund that holds a diversified portfolio of assets and trades on an exchange like a stock.

Estate Planning – The process of organizing assets and legal documents to ensure smooth transfer of wealth after death.

F

Fiduciary – A financial professional who is legally required to act in your best interest.

Financial Independence – The ability to cover living expenses without needing a traditional job, often through passive income sources.

Fixed Income – Investments, such as bonds or annuities, that provide regular, predictable returns.

G

Gross Income – Your total earnings before taxes and deductions.

Growth Stock – A company stock expected to grow at a faster rate than the overall market, usually reinvesting profits instead of paying dividends.

H

Health Savings Account (HSA) – A tax-advantaged savings account for medical expenses, available to those with a high-deductible health plan.

High-Yield Savings Account – A savings account offering a higher interest rate than a traditional bank savings account.

I

Index Fund – A type of mutual fund or ETF that tracks a market index, such as the S&P 500, for passive investing.

Inflation – The rate at which the general level of prices for goods and services rises over time, reducing purchasing power.

Individual Retirement Account (IRA) – A tax-advantaged account for retirement savings, with Traditional and Roth options.

L

Liquidity – The ease with which an asset can be converted into cash without significantly affecting its price.

Long-Term Capital Gains – Profits from selling an asset held for more than one year, usually taxed at a lower rate than short-term gains.

Low-Cost Index Fund – A passively managed fund with low fees that tracks a stock market index.

M

Municipal Bonds – Bonds issued by local governments that often provide tax-free interest income.

Mutual Fund – A pooled investment vehicle that collects money from multiple investors to buy a diversified portfolio of assets.

N

Net Worth – The total value of your assets minus your liabilities.

Non-Taxable Income – Income that is not subject to federal or state taxes, such as municipal bond interest or certain Social Security benefits.

P

Passive Income – Earnings generated with little active involvement, such as rental income, dividends, or royalties.

Portfolio – A collection of investments, including stocks, bonds, real estate, and other assets.

Pre-Tax Contributions – Money invested in retirement accounts before taxes, reducing taxable income for the year.

R

Real Estate Investment Trust (REIT) – A company that owns, operates, or finances income-generating real estate and pays investors dividends.

Required Minimum Distribution (RMD) – The minimum amount that must be withdrawn annually from tax-deferred retirement accounts after reaching a certain age.

Roth IRA – A retirement account where contributions are made with after-tax dollars, allowing tax-free withdrawals in retirement.

S

Side Hustle – A secondary source of income outside of a primary job, such as freelancing, consulting, or an online business.

Stock Market – A marketplace where investors buy and sell stocks.

Social Security – A government program that provides financial assistance to retirees and disabled individuals.

T

Tax-Advantaged Accounts – Investment accounts that offer tax benefits, such as IRAs, 401(k)s, and HSAs.

Tax Bracket – The range of income taxed at a specific rate by the government.

Traditional IRA – A tax-deferred retirement savings account where contributions reduce taxable income, but withdrawals are taxed.

Tax-Free Investment – An investment where earnings are not subject to taxation, such as Roth IRA distributions or municipal bond interest.

U

Umbrella Insurance – Extra liability insurance that provides additional protection beyond regular home or auto policies.

Universal Life Insurance – A type of permanent life insurance that includes an investment component.

V

Volatility – The measure of how much the price of an investment fluctuates over time.

Vanguard Funds – Low-cost mutual funds and ETFs known for their passive investment strategies.

W

Wealth Transfer – The process of passing assets from one generation to the next, often through estate planning.

Withholding Tax – The portion of income automatically deducted for taxes before you receive your pay check.

Recommended Resources and Further Reading

To deepen your understanding of tax-free retirement strategies, financial independence, and passive income, here are some highly recommended books, websites, and tools to help you take action.

Books on Financial Independence & Early Retirement

- **The Simple Path to Wealth** – JL Collins

  A must-read on stock market investing, simplifying financial freedom, and the power of index funds.

- **Your Money or Your Life** – Vicki Robin & Joe Dominguez

  Focuses on mindful spending, financial independence, and achieving freedom through conscious money management.

- **The Millionaire Next Door** – Thomas J. Stanley & William D. Danko

  A data-driven book revealing the habits of self-made millionaires, emphasizing frugality and smart investing.

- **Rich Dad Poor Dad** – Robert Kiyosaki

  A classic on financial education, differentiating assets from liabilities, and developing an investor mindset.

- **How to Retire Early** – Robert & Robin Charlton

A practical case study of a couple who retired in their 40s, outlining step-by-step financial strategies.

- **Die With Zero** – Bill Perkins

Encourages a shift from wealth accumulation to maximizing life experiences while ensuring financial security.

Books on Tax-Free & Passive Income Strategies

- **Tax-Free Wealth** – Tom Wheelwright

A valuable resource for understanding how tax laws can work in your favor and strategies for minimizing tax liability.

- **Investing in Dividend Stocks for Passive Income** – Troy Nelson

A step-by-step guide to building a dividend portfolio for long-term wealth generation.

- **The Book on Rental Property Investing** – Brandon Turner

Essential reading for anyone interested in real estate as a source of tax-efficient passive income.

- **The 4-Hour Workweek** – Timothy Ferriss

Covers strategies for building automated income streams, outsourcing work, and designing a lifestyle of freedom.

- **The Hands-Off Investor** – Brian Burke

A practical guide to real estate syndications for passive investors looking for hands-free income.

Websites & Online Resources

Retirement Planning & Financial Independence

- Mr. Money Mustache – Frugality and investment strategies for early retirement.

- Bogleheads – An online community dedicated to low-cost index investing and wealth-building.

- Mad Fientist – Advanced tax strategies and early retirement case studies.

Tax & Investment Planning

- IRS.gov – Official source for tax laws, deductions, and retirement contribution limits.

- SmartAsset – Free financial calculators for retirement, taxes, and investments.

- NerdWallet – Reviews and comparisons of financial products, including tax-advantaged accounts.

Stock Market & Passive Investing

- Vanguard – Low-cost index funds and ETFs for long-term investing.

- Fidelity – Investment strategies, financial tools, and tax-advantaged accounts.

- Morningstar – Fund analysis and investment research tools.

Real Estate & Alternative Investments

- BiggerPockets – A comprehensive resource on real estate investing and tax strategies.

- Fundrise – A platform for investing in real estate with a low initial investment.

- CrowdStreet – Real estate crowdfunding for accredited investors.

Recommended Tools & Calculators

- **Financial Independence Calculator** – Engaging Data
  Estimates when you can retire based on your savings rate.

- **Tax Bracket Calculator** – NerdWallet
  Helps determine your tax obligations based on income.

- **Roth vs. Traditional IRA Calculator** – SmartAsset
  Assists in deciding which retirement account best suits your financial goals.

- **Expense Tracking & Budgeting Tools – Mint, YNAB (You Need A Budget), Personal Capital**
  Useful for tracking spending and automating savings.

- **Dividend Income Tracker** – Track Your Dividends
  Helps monitor and forecast dividend income.

Made in United States
North Haven, CT
24 March 2025

67190834R00095